D1613847

CHURCHES
for the
SOUTHWEST

Ryan ~ 1/34 I   Cristo Rey Church   W. Clark

CHURCHES

for the

SOUTHWEST

THE ECCLESIASTICAL ARCHITECTURE
OF
JOHN GAW MEEM

STANFORD LEHMBERG

W. W. Norton & Company
New York • London

For information about permission to reproduce selections
from this book, write to Permissions,
W. W. Norton & Company, Inc.,
500 Fifth Avenue, New York, NY 10110

Manufacturing by KHL Printing
Book design by Abigail Sturges
Production manager: Leeann Graham

Library of Congress Cataloging-in-Publication Data
Lehmberg, Stanford E.
    Churches for the southwest : the ecclesiastical architecture of
    John Gaw Meem / Stanford Lehmberg.
        p. cm.
    Includes bibliographical references and index.
    ISBN 0-393-73182-0
    1. Meem, John Gaw, 1894---Criticism and interpretation.
    2. Church architecture—Southwest, New—20th century.
    I. Meem, John Gaw, 1894- II. Title

NA737.M438L44 2005
726.5'092—dc22

2005040665

W. W. Norton & Company, Inc.,
500 Fifth Avenue, New York, N.Y. 10110
www.wwnorton.com

W. W. Norton & Company Ltd.,
Castle House,
75/76 Wells St.,
London W1T 3QT
0 9 8 7 6 5 4 3 2 1

CONTENTS

ST. JOHN'S CATHEDRAL. Chapel.

PREFACE

JOHN GAW MEEM'S reputation as the most famous architect of New Mexico and leading exponent of the Santa Fe style is well established. Several earlier works have treated his career. The classic account by Bainbridge Bunting considers his life and works, while more recent studies discuss his role in historic preservation and the houses he designed. So far, however, there has been no book devoted primarily to the churches that were such an important part of his legacy. This book attempts to fill that gap.

I am greatly indebted to Meem's daughter, Nancy Meem Wirth, for encouraging me to undertake this project and for her continuing assistance. In particular, I am grateful to her for permission to quote from the John Gaw Meem papers housed at the Center for Southwestern Studies in the Zimmerman Library at the University of New Mexico (appropriately enough, a building designed by Meem himself) and to reproduce photographs and drawings from this archive. The members of the Center staff, especially Nancy Brown and Stella De Sa Rego, were unfailingly helpful in giving me access to the Meem job files and drawings as well as the collection of photographs of his work. Thanks to the efforts of Meem's long-time office manager, Ruth Heflin, as well as the present curators, the files are unusually full and well arranged. Others who have offered assistance include the Monsignor Jerome Martinez y Alire of St. Francis Cathedral, the Rev. Sheila Gustafson of the First Presbyterian Church, the Rev. Dale Coleman of the Church of the Holy Faith, Alfonso Trujillo of Cristo Rey, the Rev. Douglas K. Escue of Immanuel Lutheran Church, and the Rev. Lee Herring of the First Baptist Church, all of Santa Fe; Peggie Findlay, Steve Bush, Bruce Barber, and the Rev. Al Tarbell of St.

John's Cathedral in Albuquerque; Eleanor Mitchell, Roy Morgan, and Richard Schalk of Immanuel Presbyterian Church in Albuquerque; Cameron Mactavish, Dorothy Brandenburg, Barbara Brenner, and the Rev. Wayne A. Mell of the First Presbyterian Church in Taos; the Rev. Davis Given, formerly of the school and chapel at Fort Defiance, and the Rev. Jim Leehan, present rector there; the Very Rev. Lawrence J. O'Keefe, rector of Sacred Heart Cathedral in Gallup; the Rev. Canon Thomas W. Gray, rector of Grace Episcopal Church in Carlsbad; the Rev. John T. Rollinson, rector of St. James's Episcopal Church in Clovis; Brian Vallo of Acoma Pueblo; and Susan Lander of La Foret Conference and Retreat Center. To all I express my appreciation.

A note on the illustrations may be appropriate. These are of three sorts. First there are early black-and-white photographs taken by Tyler Dingee. Born in Brooklyn in 1906, Dingee moved to New Mexico and began working with Meem in 1945. He was also employed by the University of New Mexico and the laboratories at Los Alamos. He was killed by lightning on July 26, 1961, while on a fishing trip to Estes Park with his brother-in-law, the artist Will Shuster. Dingee's photographs are deposited with the Center for Southwest Research, and I am grateful for permission to reproduce them. A number of new color photographs were taken especially for this volume by my son Derek Lehmberg, who has combined a passion for photography with a career as a management consultant in the United States and Japan. Finally, I have been able to reproduce a number of drawings by Meem and members of his office, especially Edward Holien. Again, these are housed at the Center for Southwest Research. The frontispiece, an early print of Cristo Rey Church by the Santa Fe artist Willard Clark, is reproduced by kind permission of his grandson, Kevin Ryan.

READERS WHO ARE NOT FAMILIAR with the terminology for parts of a church or cathedral may find some definitions helpful. The front of the building, containing the entrance, is known as the façade. Inside there may be a narthex or gathering area. This leads into the nave or principal seating area for the congregation. The term is derived from the Latin word navis, which means ship—the nave was regarded as a ship which would carry the souls of the faithful to heaven. The altar was located in the chancel, regarded as the holiest part of the building. It was usually railed off and during the Middle Ages was not accessible to lay persons. Between the nave and the chancel was the choir (in England known as the quire), an area that accommodated singers and sometimes small congregations at services. A reredos or screen might be placed behind the altar and could be decorated with statues or painted figures of saints (in the Southwest called *santos*). Two-dimensional *santos* are called *retablos*, while three-dimensional figures are known as *bultos*. The artist who creates a santo is known as a *santero*—saint-maker—or *santera*, if female. The top of the altar traditionally was a stone slab known as a mensa. Cathedrals sometimes had an enclosed cloister—an outdoor green or garden—adjoining the building.

The ceilings of most of Meem's churches are made of wood, not stone or brick. They are supported by *vigas*, great beams which are left round like the tree trunks from which they are made.

Traditional cathedrals were built in the shape of a cross. Its side arms were known as transepts because they ran across the main axis of the building. For centuries it was usual for cathedrals to be oriented east and west, with the façade at the west end and the altar at the east, so that the congregation would face the direction of the Holy Land during services. The transepts then ran north and south. Meem's churches, however, are often not bound by this orientation: He was willing to work with the layout of areas where he was building and to accommodate existing street patterns. Nevertheless, one may still refer to the altar area as being at the liturgical east end.

CHURCH OF THE HOLY FAITH, SANTA FE. Exterior.

ONE

EARLY WORK, 1926–1939

THE UNUSUAL EVENTS of Meem's early life help us understand his special interest in the church and church architecture. He was born in 1894 in Brazil, where his father, John Gaw Meem III, was a missionary priest for the Episcopal church. Like Meems I and II he was descended from a family of Polish and German extraction that had settled in the Shenandoah Valley of Virginia in the 1830s. Most of the Meem men attended the Virginia Military Institute and studied civil engineering. John Gaw Meem II helped build a rail line in Brazil before accepting a position as architect with the U.S. Treasury Department. Meem III was also trained as an engineer but was drawn into the Episcopal ministry and in 1891 moved to Brazil, where he established a mission church in the port city of Pelotas. Here he married a Brazilian woman of German and Portuguese ancestry, Elsa Upton Krischke. John IV was their first child; three daughters and another son followed.[1]

As a teenager Meem IV returned to the United States where he too attended Virginia Military Institute. After graduation in 1914 he worked briefly for a firm that was constructing the New York subway system. With the advent of World War I he joined the army and was soon commanding a battalion and training recruits at Plattsburg, Iowa. As the war ended he was struck by the widespread influenza epidemic, but he recovered and returned to Brazil, where he worked as a credit manager for a bank in Rio de Janeiro. Weakened by his earlier illness, he soon developed tuberculosis, and the bank sent him back to New York for treatment. His doctor suggested recuperation in a sanitorium, possibly in the Southwest. When he saw an office of the Santa Fe railway proclaiming the merits of the climate in New Mexico, he purchased a ticket. Arriving in Santa Fe in 1920, he was admitted to the Sunmount Sanitorium, operated by Dr. Frank Mera. Rest, good food and good company, and nights spent on an open-air sleeping porch gradually improved his health. At Sunmount Meem made a number of friends, including Mary Vilura Conkey, who had been educated at St. Lawrence University and had taught Latin and Greek in the East. A fellow tuberculosis sufferer, she had come to Santa Fe for a cure and never left. As we will see, she encouraged Meem's interest in historic preservation and in the Episcopal church, and he built one of his finest houses for her early in his career.

Meem's interest in architecture was sparked by several new buildings designed by the local firm of Rapp and Rapp in what came to be known as the Santa Fe style.[2] When he was sufficiently recovered, Meem left Santa Fe for Denver, where he studied architecture as an apprentice with the firm Fisher and Fisher and, as a student at the Atelier Denver, with the teacher Burnham Hoyt. Hoyt was trained in Beaux-Arts architecture, not the Southwestern style that Meem was later to adopt himself, but he taught the young Meem a great deal about design.

Partly because overwork in Denver caused his health to decline, Meem returned to Santa Fe early in 1924. Again he lived at Sunmount Sanitorium. Dr. Mera made space available to him for use as an architectural studio, and he shortly opened a practice in partnership with a fellow Sunmount patient and architect, Cassius McCormick.

Some of Meem's friends were members of the Episcopal Church of the Holy Faith in Santa Fe, and they turned to him for help with the construction of a parish house. The first Episcopal priest to visit Santa Fe had come as early as 1863. Early meetings, many of them led by L. Bradford Prince as lay reader, had been conducted in the Palace of the Governors; a building in the early Gothic style was erected in 1881. It still serves as the nave of the present church. It did not, however, include space for parish meetings, classes, or offices. The leading advocate of the new building project was Mrs. Rufus J. Palen, the daughter of an Episcopal bishop and wife of one of Santa Fe's leading bankers. The Palens's daughter Caryl had recently died, tragically soon after her marriage, and the parish house was to become a memorial to her, known as Palen Hall. The exterior of Meem's design, obviously intended to harmonize with the existing stone church, displays stucco walls with half-timbered details on the façade, reminiscent of medieval English buildings. Most of the interior was simply a large meeting room that could accommodate assemblies, dinners, or classes. There was also a stage, which came to be used by the dramatic groups that flourished at the church, as well as offices, a choir room, and a kitchen. The cornerstone of Palen Hall was laid by the bishop, Frederick Howden, in 1925, and work was completed in 1926.[3]

Meem was still a young man, not yet married, when he designed Palen Hall. Shortly thereafter he was chosen as architect for a new Fine Arts Center in Colorado Springs. The principal patron of this project, Alice Bemis Taylor, introduced Meem to her niece Faith Bemis, who had studied at Vassar and had an advanced degree from the Cambridge School of Domestic and Landscape Architecture. Bemis's father was the head of the family manufacturing firm in Boston but would have preferred to build homes; her mother was the daughter of a Congregationalist minister from Colorado Springs. Because Bemis had lost her job in New York City due to the Depression, Aunt Alice suggested that she assist Meem in drafting plans for the Art Center. Bemis soon moved to Santa Fe, where she stayed with Lura Conkey until she and Meem were married (in Boston) in 1933. The Meems became enthusiastic about the church in 1940 when four English evacuees, fleeing the threat of German invasion, arrived to live with John, Faith, and their daughter Nancy. The young women were good Anglicans and wished to attend services at Holy Faith, and the Meems began to accompany them regularly.

Meem's association with Alice Taylor was also responsible for his design of the Taylor Memorial Chapel on the family estate and summer home at La Foret, in the Black Forest north of Colorado Springs. This chapel was erected by Mrs. Taylor as a memorial to her late husband. Meem completed plans and specifications after several trips to Colorado in 1929.[4] The chapel is Meem's earliest work in the Spanish mission style; it was inspired by the church at Acoma Pueblo, which (as we shall see shortly) he helped to restore. The entry is recessed between two large buttresses, which also enclose a balcony. A central pediment provides room for a single bell. The ends of large beams protrude from the side walls at two levels. The interior is dominated by an impressive reredos that was painted by Eugenie Shonnard, a friend who had first introduced Meem to Mrs. Taylor. Born in New York in 1886, Shonnard had studied with Rodin in Paris and at the New York Art Students League before settling in Santa Fe in 1926. Meem said that he regarded her as "one of the greatest sculptors in this country," and he continued to work

JOHN GAW MEEM.
His wife Faith Bemis, their daughter Nancy, and their dogs.

CHURCH OF THE HOLY FAITH.
Palen Hall.

**TAYLOR MEMORIAL CHAPEL,
LA FORET, COLORADO SPRINGS.**

TAYLOR MEMORIAL CHAPEL.
Interior with reredos (LEFT) and
balcony (ABOVE).

**TAYLOR MEMORIAL
CHAPEL.** Side door, painting
by Eugenie Shonnard.

with her for many years. The reredos includes figures of the Blessed Virgin, an archangel, and four saints—Our Lady of Guadalupe, Our Lady of Sorrows, the Benedictine nun St. Gertrude, St. Rosalia of Palermo, St. Joseph, St. Lawrence, and Raphael the Archangel. Mrs. Taylor was greatly interested in these holy figures herself and wrote a pamphlet about them, copies of which she gave to guests at her home during the 1930s. Shonnard also designed and helped execute the construction of the altar, lectern, pulpit, candle-sticks, chancel railings, and two large doorways.[5]

Meem took special care in the construction of the chapel. In particular, as he wrote Mrs. Taylor, he was concerned about the mud or adobe walls. "In California, I saw some fairly uneven ones that were plastered on cinder blocks, or something of the kind, which were very good. It looked as if they had taken a spatula and waved it over the walls, as you see the Indians do with their hands. I am terribly anxious not to get definitely square corners, etc., but you know all that already." Whatever was done in Colorado did not work well, and in August 1932 Meem had to write the contractor, George O. Teats of Rocky Ford, about repairs: Stucco was peeling off badly. "It is my feeling at the moment," he said, "that the whole of the chapel will have to be re-stuccoed because in tapping over the walls, specially around the front buttresses, it sounded hollow which means that it is only a question of time before disintegration will set in." The parapets also needed to be waterproofed. "In any case," he concluded, "we *must* make this build-ing absolutely secure against further deterioration."

Alice Taylor used the chapel for the performance of sacred music; a concert in September 1932 included works by Tchaikovsky and an anthem by Johannes Eccard for the Feast of the Presentation in the Temple. The church is now part of La Foret Conference and Retreat Center, operated by the United Church of Christ.

MARY VILURA CONKEY was also in Denver during Meem's stay there. She intro-duced him to her friend Anne Evans, whose father had been the second territorial gov-ernor of Colorado. The family was wealthy, sophisticated, and interested in art. Anne became an early patron of Colorado artists, and she was one of the first to be concerned about the preservation of the historic mission churches in the Southwest. As early as 1919 Miss Conkey, Anne Evans, and Mary Willard, another leader from Denver, formed the idea of establishing a committee that might assist with the restoration of these build-ings. They enlisted the support of Burnham Hoyt, Dr. Mera, the Santa Fe anthropolo-gist Frank Hewett, Carlos Vierra, and several other friends who shared their interests. Soon they were able to form a loosely organized Committee for the Preservation and Restoration of New Mexico Mission Churches. Archbishop Albert T. Daeger of Santa

Fe agreed to serve as chairman; Hoyt was named chief architect with Meem as his assistant. In 1932 the committee was reorganized as a society. Only a few weeks later Archbishop Daeger died as a result of a fall into an open staircase; his work in developing membership and funding was taken over by Meem's friend, Cyrus McCormick Jr.

The committee's first project, and Meem's earliest work in actual church architecture, involved the restoration of the great church at Acoma, San Estevan del Rey Mission, marvelously set on a rock in that "city of the sky."[6] It was the only Spanish mission church built before 1680 that was not destroyed in the pueblo revolt of that year. The rock and adobe for its construction had been carried in baskets up a steep 350-foot cliff, and fourteen roof beams, each 36 feet long, had been brought from the San Mateo Mountains forty miles away. Adjacent to the church was a priest's house (or *convento*), a garden, and a cemetery. But by 1920 one tower had crumbled, wood was rotting, and collapse was a distinct possibility. Burnham Hoyt made plans for restoration, including the installation of a concrete roof—which was controversial at the time and has become more so in subsequent years. Meem was placed in charge of the actual work. He would have liked to live at Acoma for several months, but Dr. Mera thought that doing so would not be good for his health; when work began in 1924, supervision was placed in the hands of Meem's friend, the artist Josef Bakos. After a year Bakos was replaced by Louis Riley, and the final stages of construction were handled by B. A. Reuter, still under Meem's supervision. The necessary materials and the salaries of the supervisors were paid for by the committee, while the work was carried out by Pueblo natives. The resident priest, Father Fridolin Shuster, supported their activities.

Meem described the work in one of his interviews with Beatrice Chauvenet:

> The church was in pretty bad shape, especially under the canales. The walls were tremendously thick—almost seven feet—and great canyons had been gouged into the side walls by the runoff water from the roof. There were two areas that particularly interested me. I wanted to see what Burnham Hoyt planned for the roof of the church that caused such severe criticism in Santa Fe. Later when I asked him about the use of concrete (he had put a cement layer on Santa Ana the year previously) he said it was needed to strengthen the roof when the Indians danced on it. I don't know whether he had ever seen them dancing on the roof— so far as I know they don't do it often—but in any case, he felt it was important to build a durable platform for them.
>
> The other thing I wanted to study was the towers. They were very dilapidated. I got quite excited when I saw that in one tower there seemed to be a central column of a wooden stairway leading to the upper story. Later when we excavated we found that this stairway had quite a unique construction. The steps each had a stub which engaged with the stub above it to form the center column, a design which to an architect was very exciting.[7]

Reuter later described the towers in a letter to the restoration committee:

These towers, from the best I could learn among the most reliable people of Acoma, were built under the supervision of a local priest, by Mexican workmen with the liberal assistance of the Indians . . . about 1902. I found their construction to consist of a conglomerate of adobe mud, adobes and rock cast together without respect to system except that it had a rock veneer; otherwise it was as if it had been cast in one piece. We had to cut it to pieces with crow bar and pick, and most of the time, according to the Indians, the wind was very cross![8]

During the last stages of restoration relations with the Pueblo Indians were strained, perhaps because of cultural differences, and it was difficult to engage the services of those who had agreed to carry out the work. Finally, in 1928 Meem wrote a detailed letter to the Pueblo governor, Juan Louis Haskey, reiterating that the committee's instructions to Reuter were "that he was to build in the best possible manner so that what was done would never have to be done over." They wanted "to be sure that the people of Acoma would have the best possible work on their church." Work was completed later that year. Meem's friends had contributed an estimated $7,000 to the project.[9]

SAN ESTEVAN DEL REY MISSION, ACOMA.

SANTA MARIA DE ACOMA,
McCARTY'S.

In 1932 Meem became involved in the design of a new church to be built at McCarty's, a site near Acoma at the intersection of the railway and Route 66, which had become a residence for members of the pueblo. Here the work was initiated by a missionary priest, Fr, Agnellus Lammert. Meem described his first meeting with Lammert in a memorandum written August 19, 1932:

> I had lunch with Father Lammert who said he has recently been assigned to the Acoma and Laguna parishes, and he is most enthusiastic about Mission architecture. He is going to build a new church at McCarty which is the summer Pueblo of Acoma. He has a very wonderful site on the mesa back of the Pueblo, and wants to put up a Church similar to Acoma, but smaller, done in the traditional manner.

Lammert showed Meem a sketch plan and asked what the Society for the Restoration and Preservation of New Mexico Mission Churches (SRPNMMC) might be able to do for him. Meem said that on behalf of the society he could furnish a set of simple plans for the construction at no cost. It all had to be done speedily because Lammert hoped to start work in two or three weeks. On August 31 Meem advised him that the lower part of the walls should be made of stone to prevent rising moisture; the rest of the building could be adobe. Meem later approved of Lammert's decision to put in concrete foundations and agreed that concrete blocks might be used for the chimneys. When Meem's drawings arrived in September, Lammert wrote, "I do not know when I ever felt so happy as this morning when the plans you so kindly made came to me. I simply cannot express my appreciation." The exterior walls of the handsome building are, in fact, entirely of stone, and the façade is capped by twin towers reminiscent of those at Acoma. Meem later sent drawings of the decorations on the old beams at Acoma, hoping that they would "suggest decorative ideas to the Indian carvers." Some complications did arise, especially when a preservation society in the East (not Meem's group) withdrew its offer to provide $2,500 on the grounds that they did not like the idea of a replica of the old Acoma church—they would have preferred something in the California Mission style. In the end the Eastern society did contribute $1,000, and some additional costs were borne by the SRPNMMC.

In March 1933 Lammert said that he would have a hundred men on the job for a few days, while about ten would stay on to complete the work. That fall he was able to report that the workers had finished carving the beams and corbels according to Meem's plans. Meem and his new wife were invited to the dedication service of Santa Maria Mission chapel at McCarty's on Thanksgiving Day 1933, followed by a luncheon at the Yucca Hotel in Grants.[10]

Meem was less directly involved in Lammert's restoration of the church at Laguna and was unhappy that cement plaster rather than the traditional adobe had been used. Lammert replied that "the younger generation got tired of plastering it with mud each year. . . . If we had not done something the old place would have caved in one of these years." In 1936 Meem provided Lammert with drawings for the façade of the chapel at Mesita, which was to have a simple front with a bell at the top, and he advised Lammert about the mission chapels at Paraje and Acomita, near Acoma on Route 66. "The Indians have surely done wonders at Paraje," Lammert told him. Paraje is part of Laguna Pueblo. Its church, strikingly situated at the foot of a range of mountains, is reminiscent of the earlier building at Laguna but smaller in size and darker in color. There are no towers, though a bell hangs over the entrance. The mission at Acomita was dependent on Acoma both administratively and stylistically. It is made of adobe with twin towers and a balcony above the doors. Like McCarty's it has remarkable carvings on all the ceiling beams as well as the balcony.

In 1938 Meem corresponded with Father Jose Garcia at the famous church of Ranchos de Taos: He was delighted that Garcia was replastering the old church with mud, and "doing it by the old fashioned methods, that is, by using women who, traditionally, have always done this type of work." Several years earlier he had provided plans for a proposed church of Franciscan Friars at Shiprock.[11]

At about the same time Meem worked with Archbishop Rudolph Gerken, who had succeeded Daeger, and the SRPNMMC to rebuild the church of Santo Tomás in Abiquiú, the village later made famous by its association with Georgia O'Keeffe. Here the first church had been built in the 1750s, shortly after the area was settled by American Indians living under Spanish rule, known as Genízaros. This building partially burned in the 1880s and was replaced by a second church, but it had become ruined by the 1930s.

In 1932 Abiquiú was part of the parish of El Rito, where the priest was a young German immigrant, William Bickhaus. Bickhaus had been an ambulance driver in the German army. After the war he had come to the United States, where he soon became involved in missionary work and teaching. He was also interested in the preservation and restoration of historic churches and assumed leadership of a movement to put up a new church in Abiqiú. Bickhaus admired Meem's Mission Revival style and asked him to design the building.

Meem's plans were completed in 1935, and the old church was demolished. All the labor for the construction was volunteered by men from the village and region. Some building materials were provided by the restoration society, but 48,000 adobe bricks

**SAN JOSÉ MISSION,
LAGUNA.** (LEFT).

**SAINT MARGARET MARY
CHURCH, PARAJE.** (BELOW).

SAINT ANNE CHURCH, ACOMITA. (LEFT).

SANTO TOMÁS, ABIQUIÚ. (BELOW).

were made of the local soil by the local workers. None of the materials from the old building was reused; some vigas were saved but put into a dance hall rather than the new church. The only controversy that arose—it was to become a bitter one—concerned the orientation of the building. Traditionalists insisted that it should occupy the same site as its predecessors, facing south, but Meem, Bickhaus, and Archbishop Gerken favored a more liturgical east–west orientation. Construction of an east-facing church began, but almost immediately one of the native residents rammed his Model T Ford repeatedly into the foundations, damaging them beyond repair. When work resumed the volunteers workers repoured a foundation facing south, and the church was completed with that focus. In other ways as well, Meem's plans were ignored. He did not supervise the construction—Bickhaus took that upon himself—and when work was finished in 1937, the architect declined to attend the dedication ceremonies. Despite these problems, the church does reflect Meem's style, both in its façade and in its interior. Its beautifully carved beams and corbels were made by students at the Works Progress Administration (WPA) training school in El Rito, perhaps working from drawings by Meem.[12]

Meem and members of the restoration society were also responsible for the transfer of the Santuario de Chimayó from private hands to Catholic Archdiocese of Santa Fe. Famous for the healing qualities attributed to its earth, which was preserved in a hole in the floor and could be spread on ailing bodies, this private chapel dating from the early nineteenth century was threatened by decay and by the danger that it might fall into the hands of an unscrupulous promoter. At the request of Archbishop Daeger, Meem discussed the situation with members of the society. Although they themselves did not have the necessary funds for the purchase of the church, they did find an anonymous donor, secured through the efforts of George Day, treasurer of Yale University. The final price was $6,000 (above the original offer), and the owners, evidently fearing that a check might not be good, demanded to be paid cash in twenty-dollar bills. Ownership was transferred in October 1929 at a ceremony held in the archbishop's garden in Santa Fe. A photograph of the scene shows Meem himself handing the certificate of title to the archbishop.[13] Under Meem's leadership the society had also assisted with the restoration of the church at Las Trampas. Despite the reluctance of some residents to cooperate with outsiders, they succeeded in putting on a new roof and, some years later, erecting the present "saucy little towers" designed by Meem.[14] Meem summarized the accomplishments of the preservation society in a letter to Archbishop Gerken, dated November 28, 1934: Total expenditures between 1919 and 1934 had exceeded $17,000.[15]

Working in a rather different vein, Meem designed a chapel at the Bonnell Ranch in Glencoe, New Mexico, in 1933. This was a project initiated by the Rev. Frederick B. Howden Jr., son of the Episcopal bishop and himself rector of St. Andrew's Church in Roswell. As the younger Howden wrote Meem, "At Bonnell's ranch near Glencoe we have a mission of mountaineer people who are desirous at this time of obtaining an attractive chapel." A beautiful site was offered—it was just east of Ruidoso and surrounded by the Lincoln National Forest—and it was hoped that with volunteer labor the work might be completed for $500. Meem's reply was delayed by his honeymoon and then by an attack of appendicitis, but he did send a set of plans. Within a year local workers had completed the chapel, which was dedicated on June 3, 1934. Howden urged Meem to attend the ceremony, adding, "You will recall that you were kind enough to contribute a sketch for this enterprise. We have tried to follow out the details of that sketch accurately, and all who have inspected the Chapel are delighted with it."[16]

Another of Meem's early buildings is the Laboratory of Anthropology in Santa Fe. Although it is not a church, the exterior of its lounge wing was obviously inspired by Pueblo churches: the façade has what appear to be large adobe buttresses (they are, in fact, hollow and are made of blocks covered with stucco), and the rear displays a large buttress similar to that at Ranchos de Taos. A commission had been held in 1929 to select the architect; committee members, who included Sylvanus Morley, Dr. Frank Mera, Amelia White, and Mary Cabot Wheelwright, chose Meem over such competitors as Cram and Ferguson of Boston and William Penhallow Henderson of Santa Fe. The building was completed in 1930.[17]

BETWEEN 1935 AND 1940 Meem was involved in major structural repairs to St. Francis Cathedral, the great church erected in Santa Fe by Bishop Lamy in the 1860s. Chunks of plaster had fallen from the ceiling, the roof vaults were cracking, piers were splitting, and there was a large crack in the façade between the entrance and the rose window. Excavation revealed that the foundations were inadequate and that the vaulting had been shoddily constructed of inferior materials. As Meem wrote, the whole structure was in "immediate danger." He added, "The cracks in the ceiling haunted [Lamy's assistant and successor] Machebeuf to the hour of his death." The towers, too, were poorly constructed, and Meem did not believe that they could ever support the additional stories that had been planned. At most, they might be capped by wooden spires.

By January 1936 the Grill Mill (Fred Grill's construction firm) had completed repairs to the roof and ceiling, with new steel beams and some restuccoing, at a cost of

SAN JOSÉ, LAS TRAMPAS.

$9,687.71. In 1940 about $21,000 more had to be spent to repair the columns and enlarge their footings. The work was so serious that the floor of the cathedral had to be removed and services had to be transferred to the gymnasium of St. Michael's College for several months. In his final report, written in 1941, Meem concluded that "owing to the age of the building and to the inferior quality of stone masonry, both material and workmanship, additional upkeep and repair may be expected even though the major repairs of the 1935–41 period have corrected the worst defects." The total cost of the project was only about $35,000; that Meem had been able to do so much work at such a low cost, even during the years of the Depression, was a minor miracle. Meem's office

ST. FRANCIS CATHEDRAL, SANTA FE. Restoration.

would normally have charged a fee of 6 percent for supervision, but because of his sympathy and concern he reduced the charge to 5 percent. Archbishop Gerken was very appreciative of his efforts and continued to consult him about all the building projects of the Catholic Church in New Mexico.[18] Few of those who admire the cathedral today realize that without Meem's work, it might have fallen down.

MEEM'S WORK in restoring New Mexico missions had prepared him for the design of his finest church in this style and his best known piece of ecclesiastical architecture, the church of Cristo Rey on Upper Canyon Road in Santa Fe. The story that lies behind this project is fascinating.

The saga goes back to the year 1760, when the Spanish governor of New Mexico, Francisco Marín del Valle, decided to erect a military chapel, known as La Castrense, on the south side of the Santa Fe plaza. The three-foot-thick walls were made of adobe, with carved ornaments of white limestone. The most important feature of the chapel was its reredos, carefully described in an early report written by Fray Francisco Domínguez:

> The altar screen is all of white stone. . . . It consists of three sections. In the center of the first, as if enthroned, is an ordinary oil painting on canvas with a painted frame of Our Lady of Light, which was brought from Mexico at the aforesaid Governor Marin's expense. . . . On the right side of this image is St. Ignatius of Loyola, and on the left St. Francis Solano. Toward the middle of the second section is St. James the Apostle, and beside him St. Joseph on the right and St. John Nepomuck on the left. The third section has only Our Lady of Valvanera, and the Eternal Father at the top. All these images, with the exception of Our Lady of Light, are in medallions of the same stone of which the altar is made and carved in high relief, painted as is suitable, and this work resembles a copy of the façades which are now used in famous Mexico.[19]

It has been called "the finest piece of ecclesiastical sculpture in America [dating] from Spanish colonial times."[20]

By 1832 the building was in bad repair, and when Americans first arrived in 1846 they found its condition appalling. For a time they used it as an ammunition storehouse, and in 1851 the chief justice of the territory ordered that it be turned into a courtroom. This greatly distressed the Spanish settlers, who appealed to Bishop Lamy and his Vicar Machebeuf. For a few years La Castrense was used as the bishop's chapel, but his interests centered on the construction of the new cathedral that would replace the old parish church or Parroquia. In 1859 Lamy sold the land adjoining La Castrense to Levi Spiegelberg, one of Santa Fe's leading merchants, and in 1860 he turned over what

remained of the building itself to another merchant, Simon Delgado. New trading establishments were erected on the site. The only object saved was the extraordinary reredos, which was placed behind the main altar of La Parroquia. Later, when the new cathedral was complete and the old parish church was torn down, it was stored in an obscure spot behind the eastern apse as part of a museum that also contained Lamy's red velvet chair and a number of elaborate vestments.

In 1934 it was proposed that a chapel to house the reredos be added to St. Francis cathedral. Meem wrote Archbishop Gerken that the SPRNMMC would support such a project, and a leaflet appealing for funds was published. This leaflet listed more than fifty influential sponsors, including Archbishop Daeger and Governor Bronson Cutting, as well as Andrew W. Mellon.[21] Measurements of the reredos had been made by Faith Bemis, then a member of Meem's office and not yet his wife.

CRISTO REY, SANTA FE.
Exterior.

CRISTO REY. Interior with historic reredos as originally planned (LEFT) and today (BELOW).

But fund raising for the chapel was not successful, in part because of the nation-wide economic depression, and in any case, Archbishop Gerken soon developed another plan. As he surveyed the churches of his diocese, he concluded that a new parish was needed to serve those who lived on the east side of Santa Fe, on Upper Canyon Road and Cerro Gordo. The construction could serve as a means of celebrating the four hundredth anniversary of Coronado's entry into the country, and it could offer a fine setting for the reredos. At a dinner held on April 6, 1939, the archbishop announced his project, and he mentioned it again during the Easter services in the cathedral. He appointed one of his clergy, the Rev. Daniel Krahe, as head of the new parish and supervisor of the construction, and he contacted Meem's office for architectural plans. Meanwhile the Archbishop purchased the necessary land on Upper Canyon Road from three related owners, James Catanach, Enrique Sena, and David Rodriguez Sr., the last of whom, aged ninety, was to become the oldest member of the new parish. They accepted a payment much lower than the actual value of the land, because they and their neighbors were eager to have a church nearby.

Meem's design incorporated a number of elements derived from the mission churches he had helped restore. A low tower is reminiscent of one at Acoma. The balconied façade is similar to that at Las Trampas. A transverse clerestory that provided illumination for the altar and reredos had been a feature of many of the older buildings. A portal stretching along the north side of the building is similar to one Meem designed earlier for the church at McCarty's. The church was to be constructed of traditional materials: adobe bricks and great wood *vigas*. Groundbreaking took place on April 26, 1939, very soon after Gerken announced the project. It had been planned that the archbishop would lay the first two adobe bricks, but some souvenir hunter made off with one of them (it has never been recovered) and Gerken had to make do with putting only one in place. The first wheelbarrow of cement for the foundation was poured by Father Krahe on June 1.

Cristo Rey church and its attached rectory form a continuous building 350 feet long. A total of 180,000 adobe bricks were used in its walls. There was some discussion about adding straw to the clay used in the bricks; Meem said that it was traditional and would strengthen them. Local workmen—Krahe lists 123 of them in his book about the church—made the bricks, using materials from the site itself. At the height of construction they were able to produce as many as 4,800 bricks a day. The roof was constructed of 222 native pine *vigas*, some of them 45 feet long, which were suspended from steel girders not visible from below. The largest girder above the sanctuary beam weighs 5,500 pounds. The foundation for the reredos is a solid block of concrete 15 feet by 32

CRISTO REY. Ceiling and corbels.

feet. The length of the church proper is 155 feet. The height of the nave to the split cedar ceiling is 27 feet, while the sanctuary is 32 feet high. The tower, including the cross that crowns it, rises 52 feet. There are two transepts and two sacristies. The exterior walls are tied together with three bands of reinforced concrete.

One of those who made the mud bricks was Alfonso Trujillo, often called "Trompo." A member of one of the families that had owned the land, he was seventeen years old at the time. More than fifty years later he remembered the events very well. "We worked like horses and didn't even get tired," he said; "it was hard work but it was fun." The workers were paid $2 a day, which, as Trujillo said, was "not bad" for those days.[22]

Under each beam there are four handcarved corbels. As Krahe noted, "Most of the labor was done by the natives; a few skilled carpenters were used for finish work." The carved doors and other wooden fittings were executed by boys at the diocesan Lourdes Trade School in Albuquerque. As before, Meem employed Fred Grill to supervise construction, although he visited the site frequently himself. The building was finished very

CRISTO REY. Balcony (ABOVE)
and detail (RIGHT).

rapidly; it was blessed by Archbishop Gerken on June 27, 1940, and immediately opened for services.[23]

In a letter written in 1953 to Paul Kalemen, who was preparing an article about the reredos, Meem described its installation in detail:

> At the time the reredos was moved in 1939, the broken panel of Our Lady of Light was on the floor leaning against the adobe altar. Since it was of the same workmanship as the other panels, and had the same type of border, it seemed obvious that at one time it might have belonged to it. It fitted the central panel with the exception of the top which was level, whereas the niche was semi-hexagonal. However, the niche at some time in the past was altered to its present shape with very crude masonry.
>
> The color of the Lady panel was different as if it had been weathered, showing that it had been used elsewhere than in the reredos. But the fact that the panel was found near the reredos, was similar to the other panels in it, and that it might originally have belonged to it, made us hesitate to separate them.
>
> We therefore simply rested the panel in the niche, without any attempt to fix it in place, thus making possible her easy removal should future research determine that she never belonged to the reredos.[24]

As interior fittings were added a controversy arose over the Stations of the Cross. On the recommendation of Faith's aunt, Miss Marjorie Gregg of South Tamworth, New Hampshire, Meem had secured a group of prints from the Rev. T. Heminway of Sherburne, Vermont. "It had been our thought," he wrote Heminway, "to use these prints in a new Roman Catholic Church which I built last year here in Santa Fe." The reinstalled reredos, he explained,

> is a magnificent eighteenth century piece of stone sculpture. It is so rich that all other items of equipment, including the Stations, should be kept subordinate. I felt sure the priest in charge would approve my recommendation, but when I showed him the prints, he felt that everything in the church should be made locally. . . . In theory I think he is right, but in practice it would be so much better to have these lovely prints on the walls.

He was afraid that some second-rate set of wood carvings would be used. A letter to Aunt Marjorie explains that it was the archbishop who insisted on original local work; "he would not approve of prints which might be found in another church."[25]

Despite this disagreement, Archbishop Gerken was most appreciative of Meem's work and of the fact that he had not charged the diocese the normal fees for his time and office overhead. "I wish to assure you," he wrote in January 1940, "that I appreciate the donation of your time and overhead very much on the Cristo Rey Church job. I pray that this may be a source of great consolation to you and that it will bring you added glory and power and of course much publicity in your wonderful field of work." [26]

When Beatrice Chauvenet interviewed Meem in 1977 he reminisced about visiting Cristo Rey with the archbishop. Gerken had said, "John, let's go up in the south tower, and see how well the church fits its setting." When they did so Gerken expressed his pleasure in the work their thought, hands, and prayer had wrought:

"You would make a good Catholic, John," he said quietly.

"Your Grace, I am a Catholic," Meem said. "My father was an Anglican priest in Brazil, and I belong to Holy Faith Episcopal Church."

The Archbishop smiled. "Yes," he said, "You are one of us." [27] Indeed Meem was made an honorary member of the parish.

"All in all the church is an architectural gem," one of Meem's friends in the SRPN-MMC agreed. [28] The parish celebrated its fiftieth anniversary with a number of special events in 1990.

ALTHOUGH IT IS NOT A CHURCH, Zimmerman Library on the campus of the University of New Mexico in Albuquerque reveals the influence of the Pueblos and their churches. The exterior, plastered to resemble adobe, was inspired by the appearance of Taos Pueblo, and the interior has a number of details borrowed from early churches. The most notable of these is the ceiling of what is now known as the West Wing Reading Room. A replica of the ceiling of the church at Ranchos de Taos, it has elegantly carved corbels supporting a series of small *vigas*. The library, which opened in April 1938, remains one of Meem's finest structures and is the chief monument to his long career as University architect.

MEEM'S LAST CHURCH of the 1930s was the new building for the First Presbyterian Church in Santa Fe. This was one of the oldest Protestant congregations in New Mexico. As early as 1866 the Rev. David McFarland had been sent to Santa Fe by the Board of Domestic Missions of the Presbyterian Church. Like the Episcopalians, he held services for a time in the Palace of the Governors, but the Presbyterians soon purchased the remains of a church on Grant Avenue, near the plaza. This church had been built several decades earlier by the Baptists, but they shortly abandoned their work in Santa Fe as hopeless. The rebuilt church, dominated by a large square tower, was modernized and gothicized by the Presbyterians in 1882. [29]

Meem was first approached to design a manse adjoining the church. As he told his Presbyterian friends several decades later,

**FIRST PRESBYTERIAN
CHURCH, SANTA FE.**

The First Presbyterian Church of Santa Fe has been a patron and enthusiastic supporter of
the regional Spanish Pueblo style of architecture ever since they commissioned me in 1927
to make preliminary drawings for the Presbyterian Manse. [That was] just three years after I
started to practice architecture, which means that your interest in me and in my architectural firm has been practically co-extensive with my practice. It has been a relationship I have
greatly cherished.[30]

The church itself was rebuilt to Meem's plans in 1939. Once again his recollections
are of interest. The preliminary problem, he said, was

what to do with the existing red brick church with its ungainly tower on the southeast corner of the façade. The temptation was to include the walls, which were in a good state of

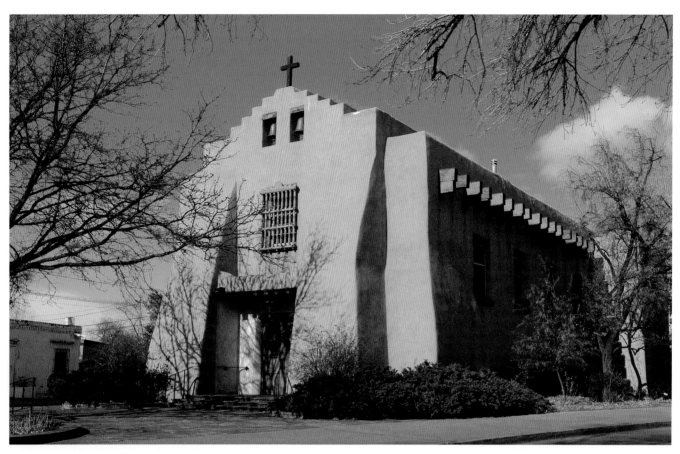

**FIRST PRESBYTERIAN
CHURCH, SANTA FE.** Exterior
and original plan (FACING PAGE)
showing tower on the side.

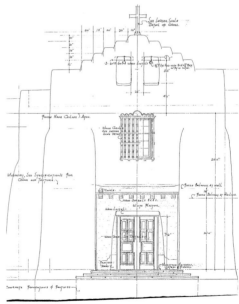

**FIRST PRESBYTERIAN
CHURCH.** Final plan for entrance.

PERSPECTIVE

SECOND FLOOR PLAN

GROUND FLOOR PLAN

PROPOSED NEW BUILDING FOR
THE FIRST PRESBYTERIAN CHURCH AT SANTA FE
MEEM AND MCCORMICK ARCHITECTS · SANTA FE, NEW MEXICO

preservation, into the design of the new Church. I even made a drawing, using this tower and trying to soften it to conform with the style we wanted, but the result was not good—in fact it was abysmal. So, we decided to start fresh and take out the old walls, foundations and all, but to reuse the bricks after cleaning them.

A surviving drawing from Meem's files, dated 1938, shows how his abortive design would have worked. The principal entrance would have been just to the right of the preserved bell tower, where people appear in the sketch. The accompanying floor plan shows that the choir, altar, and pulpit would have been at the south end of the building—the opposite of the present arrangement—with a lower ceiling than the main seating area and without the door and buttresses that now provide the church's main façade.

In the end Meem reversed the orientation of what was called the auditorium and chose a simple floor plan similar to that of the church at Acoma. The design of the ceiling was determined by the size of available wood beams. These rest on corbels whose profiles are similar to those of the bolsters in the patio of the house of El Greco in Toledo, Spain, and are a vivid reminder of the Spanish origins of our regional style. The cor-

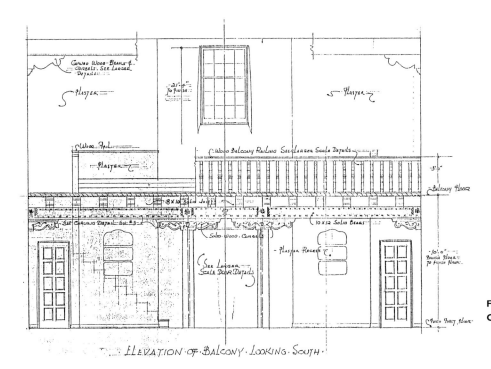

ELEVATION OF BALCONY LOOKING SOUTH

FIRST PRESBYTERIAN CHURCH. Drawing for balcony.

bels rest on a plate mould carved with a pattern symbolizing the rope associated with with St. Francis' costume. Above the beams, the ceiling is made of aspen poles laid close together as in the ancient proto-type [*sic*] still to be seen at Chaco Canyon which supported the earth roof on a layer of reeds and grasses.

Meem thought that the façade "reminds one of the Church of San Jose in Laguna Pueblo, but actually is very different with its two great buttresses." It is also very similar to the entrance Mcem had designed a decade earlier for the Taylor Memorial Chapel. The exterior is adobe colored but is actually made of brick and tile covered with permanent stucco, because Meem felt that true adobe was too difficult to maintain. Financial considerations necessitated the omission of the balcony and wood grilles over the windows from the original building, but these were later added, and the carvings on the balcony are among the principal beauties of the building. It is said that some of the construction was undertaken by prisoners who were released from the local jail during the day in order to work on the church. Meem's office actually suffered a loss of $387.72 on the project, but he said that he regarded this as a contribution "to the good cause."

FIRST PRESBYTERIAN CHURCH. Balcony.

The manse had been built during the pastorate of the Rev. Paul Reiter. The church was begun under A. G. Tozer and was completed under the Rev. Kenneth Keeler, who also commissioned Meem to design Hart Hall in 1949. This addition, which adjoined the church, provided space for classes and meetings.

During a large building campaign in 2004, all the church buildings except the sanctuary were torn down and replaced by new spaces for offices, education, and a day-care center. Meem's sanctuary was preserved and given better lighting, so that the carved details could be seen and appreciated more easily. Acoustics were also improved. The

FIRST PRESBYTERIAN CHURCH. Balcony railing (ABOVE) and (LEFT) detail of corbel.

front wall was pushed back about eight feet to make room for a new pipe organ, a fine instrument made by C. B. Fisk. Although this addition did alter the appearance of the sanctuary, it harmonized well with Meem's work The Rev. Sheila Gustafson was pastor at the time of this major project, which cost more than six million dollars.

The Presbyterian church and Cristo Rey were among John Gaw Meem's finest works of the 1930s. As the decade ended and he celebrated his forty-fifth birthday, he was firmly established as the leading church architect in New Mexico, perhaps in the entire Southwest.

ST. JOHN'S CATHEDRAL, ALBUQUERQUE. Original plan for expansion (TOP) and final plan for rebuilding (BOTTOM).

TWO

THE MIDDLE YEARS, 1940–1951

ALTHOUGH ANY ATTEMPT to divide John Gaw Meem's design of churches into periods may be artificial, it still helps to consider his work more or less chronologically. Here we examine the ecclesiastical architecture of his middle years, the decade of the 1940s with a slight extension into the early 1950s. The fact that this was the time of World War II naturally meant that church building was delayed, but several of Meem's finest buildings had been designed, if not completed, by 1951. We begin with what eventually became one of Meem's greatest works, the Cathedral of St. John in Albuquerque.

The first Episcopal service in Albuquerque took place in 1875, twelve years later than the earliest gathering in Santa Fe. It was conducted by the Rt. Rev. William Forbes Adams, who had recently been named bishop of the new Missionary District of New Mexico and Arizona. After meeting for a time in hotels, the Albuquerque Episcopalians built their first church at the corner of Silver Avenue and Fourth Street, where three lots had been purchased for $310. Although some members said that the church should be called St. John's in the Fields because it was several blocks from Central Avenue, the site was actually close to the business district that was developing near the new railroad tracks. The Rev. Henry Forrester, who had been Bishop Adams' chaplain, was largely responsible for promoting construction. Friends in the East as well as members of the congregation raised $5,000. Arizona sandstone was given by the Atlantic and Pacific

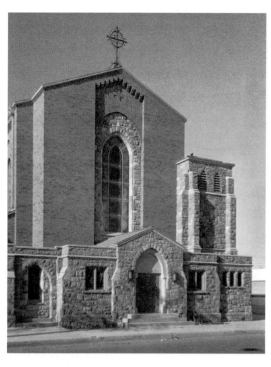

ST. JOHN'S CATHEDRAL.
Façade (LEFT) and exterior
(BELOW).

ST. JOHN'S CATHEDRAL.
Interior.

ST. JOHN'S CATHEDRAL.
Drawing for chapel.

Railroad, which was using it for its own buildings. The church, like Holy Faith in Santa Fe, was in the simplified Early English Gothic style, with lancet windows lighting its nave. A large low tower provided access to the church from Fourth Avenue. One stained-glass window was installed, in memory of a parishioner's mother. Thirty-three communicants attended the first service of the mission on November 5, 1882.[1]

Debt plagued the church for a several years but was finally paid off in 1894. In 1900 the mission attained parish status, and a year later an adjacent house was acquired as a rectory. In 1906 Bishop John Mills Kendrick described St. John's as "one of our most churchly buildings . . . an ornament to the town and a credit to the congregation." It was his successor, the Rt. Rev. Frederick B. Howden, who determined that St. John's should serve as the cathedral for the Missionary District of New Mexico and Southwest Texas. It supplanted the cathedral at El Paso in 1927.

ST. JOHN'S CATHEDRAL. Chapel.

Meem's first involvement with St. John's came in 1930, when he was commissioned to build a Cathedral House that would house the administrative offices of the diocese as well as providing classrooms for the cathedral parish. The contract price was $64,878; Meem reduced his usual fee from 5 percent to 4 percent to indicate his support of the work. The exterior was made of stone that matched the stone used in the cathedral, again provided by the railroad. The entrance to the cathedral and Cathedral House was moved from Fourth Street to Silver Avenue, where a narthex and cloister with pointed Gothic arches were constructed. The existing tower was heightened and a spire added.[2]

By the 1940s it was evident that the church was not large enough for the growing congregation. Bishop James M. Stoney, who had assumed office in 1942, helped establish a fund for remodeling and expansion. In September 1944 Dean Douglas Matthews wrote Meem that he wished to talk with him about the enlargement of the church, but

ST. JOHN'S CATHEDRAL. Interior, looking toward entrance (ABOVE) and chancel (RIGHT).

ST. JOHN'S CATHEDRAL.
Windows above altar.

"there is no desperate hurry as we shall not be able to build until the war is over." The following year saw the installation of a new dean, the Very Rev. Lloyd W. Clarke, who shared Stoney's vision and wished to move forward as rapidly as possible. The architectural firm of Meem, Zehner, Holien and Associates was retained to make plans, with Meem himself assuming personal responsibility, even though he was "swamped by work just now." At first it was thought that the existing building might be retained and enlarged; correspondence in Meem's files discusses this possibility and a surviving drawing illustrates Meem's earliest proposal. This would have kept the old church and tower, added transepts and a new chancel area, and crowned the building with a tall, slim spire. But it soon became apparent that it would be better to demolish the existing church and start afresh. A memorandum describes a meeting in which Meem was joined by Bishop Stoney, Dean Clarke, and five other church leaders. They agreed to take down the existing building and erect a new cathedral with a seating capacity of six hundred. The narthex and arcade connecting the church and Cathedral House would be retained. The tower might be kept or not, but "the general opinion seemed to be that it was not worth saving." The stone in the existing building was to be reused if this did not prove too costly. A side chapel was deemed desirable but not essential. The church was to be 40 feet wide; this meant that it had to be at least 40 feet high "in order to achieve a feeling of loftiness inside the building." It was hoped that the cost of construction could be capped at $300,000, of which Meem offered to contribute $1,000 himself.[3]

A second drawing depicts the cathedral as built. The tower was, in fact, retained—actually, it was dismantled and then rebuilt—and the idea of transepts with a spire was dropped. Existing stone was reused for the side entrance and the façade, but the rest of the exterior was constructed, less expensively, of red brick, carefully chosen to harmonize with the stone. The Gothic style once again derives from thirteenth-century English churches, though according to a long-time member of St. John's, Meem himself stressed the influence of cathedrals in southern France. The nave and chancel do indeed convey the sense of loftiness that Meem wanted. The six-bay nave has low side aisles, separated from the main seating area by a colonnade of tall pointed arches. The piers are octagonal and have plain capitals, unadorned by sculpture or the classical orders. The floor is marble. Colored panels between the wood beams of the roof are similar to those in the English parish church at Long Melford in Suffolk. A drawing made as late as 1952 shows how the side chapel to the right of the high altar was intended to look. Bainbridge Bunting regretted that Meem had not retained the original nave, for he felt that "the plain stucco walls in an interior as vast as the present cathedral are less comforting than they were at the intimate scale of the old church that was replaced."[4] It is hard to share this opinion. Today the stained-glass windows admit beautifully colored light into the church, recently installed Stations of the Cross created by the Santa Fe artist Marie Romero Cash add interest to the side aisles, and the ample spaces provide an ideal setting for liturgical processions.

No detail was too small for Meem's consideration. The files contain correspondence with A. G. Sabol, head of the Reuter Organ Company in Lawrence, Kansas, concerning the installation of an appropriate pipe organ. Most of the leading organ builders, including Schantz (E. M. Skinner was then its tonal director), M. P. Möller, and Casavant, were considered. Meem suggested that the existing small pipe organ in Albuquerque might be purchased by Holy Faith in Santa Fe, which was using an electronic instrument, but nothing came of this possibility. Both the Judson Studios of Los Angeles and Connick Associates of Boston were consulted about stained-glass windows; in the end the contract was awarded to Connick, the company that had made the great east rose window for the Cathedral of St. John the Divine in New York City, as well as windows for Grace Cathedral in San Francisco, Princeton University Chapel, St. John's Cathedral in Denver, and the Fourth Presbyterian Church on Michigan Avenue in Chicago. Meem was personally involved in determining the symbolism embodied in the windows. In 1954 he wrote Orin E. Skinner, the head of Connick, saying, "Your 'beginning' window over the narthex of the Cathedral of St. John in Albuquerque is very beautiful and adds immeasurably to the religious quality of the Church. Thank you." Here the top panel shows God blessing his people, the center section is a nativity scene with figures of Joseph and Mary, and the lower panel depicts the baptism of Jesus by John the Baptist.

Among the other windows designed by Connick are the three lancets above the altar. All of these are memorials; the one on the west was originally given anonymously—its inscription does not state a donor—but Meem later acknowledged that he had paid for it himself as a memorial to missionaries, especially his father. As Dean Clarke wrote Meem, "We will share with you the thrill and deep satisfaction behind this gift." The architect also made detailed plans for pews, kneelers, hymn boards, and for the use of stenciling to provide ornamental patterns on some walls. When a sound system was installed, it was agreed that the acoustics of the building were exceptionally good.

The cornerstone had been laid on November 25, 1951, and construction was completed very speedily. Robert E. McKee was the general contractor. The cathedral was dedicated at a grand evening service on November 11, 1952, with Presiding Bishop Henry Knox Sherrill present to assist Bishop Stoney and Dean Clarke. Naturally the architect also attended. Two years later Dean Clarke announced that he was leaving Albuquerque to accept a position at Trinity Church in Watertown, New York. In a letter dated December 3, 1954, Meem wrote Clarke, "You and I had a great adventure together in the construction of the Cathedral and I like to think one reason it turned out to be so beautiful is because of your tolerance and understanding and our mutual friendship." Clarke responded, "I am very happy that you also feel that the adventure of building the Cathedral in which many people shared was especially an adventure for the two of us. I had the feeling all along that our close relationship in this had a great deal to do with what we accomplished."[5]

In later years there were suggestions that the cathedral should be relocated to a suburban site where more space would be available, but it was decided that it should remain "in the heart of the city as a symbol of the unity of Christians." (The words were those of Dean John Haverland.) It did become necessary, however, to modernize the Cathedral House. This was done in 1974, after Meem's retirement, by John McHugh, a Santa Fe architect who had worked in Meem's office. Meem's stone façade was left standing, but the interior was completely rebuilt so that there were new offices, a large hall named for Anna Kaseman, a parishioner whose bequest had paid for much of the work, and spaces for youth, music, and community outreach. Meem's style and spirit remain dominant.

In 1949 St. John's assisted in establishing another Episcopal congregation in Albuquerque—the church of St. Mark's-on-the-Mesa, to be located in University Heights to the east of the University of New Mexico campus. This was a project of Bishop Stoney and Dean Clarke, who believed that St. John's was filled to overflowing and a new mission was needed. Some parishioners from the cathedral were virtually ordered to transfer to St. Mark's, and St. John's provided substantial financial assistance for its building. Meem drew up plans and specifications for a parish house designed in the Adobe Mission style, where services would be held until it became feasible to build the church proper, and he gave amazing attention to details, even specifying the doors on the boys' toilets. A contract signed in 1949 gave the initial cost as $51,492.87. Bishop Stoney was appreciative of Meem's work, but correspondence between Meem and the Rev. G. P. La Barre, the priest at St. Mark's, indicates that not all vestry members wanted Meem as the architect or his Southwest Pueblo style as the form of the church. Another architect was chosen when the church was expanded.[6]

The architect's services to St. John's were commemorated by a John Gaw Meem Day, held at the cathedral on August 22, 1976. Meem himself read the Epistle, a portion of St. Paul's letter to the Corinthians, which spoke about the master builder laying firm foundations. A gala reception followed, and retrospective exhibitions of Meem's work were displayed at the public library as well as at the church.[7]

**CHURCH OF THE HOLY
FAITH, SANTA FE.** Drawing
for choir and chancel
(LEFT) and interior (ABOVE).

THE CHURCH OF THE HOLY FAITH in Santa Fe received Meem's attention at the same time he was working for the cathedral in Albuquerque.[8] As we have seen, he had designed Palen Hall in 1925. In 1940 a new sacristy and office for the rector were added to the rear of the hall and a new altar was placed in the church. Two years later a gift in memory of Bishop Howden, who had recently died, was designated for a reredos to be placed above the altar. An impressive work that still dominates the interior of Holy Faith, it was designed by Wilfred Edwards Anthony of New York City but was actually carved by one of Santa Fe's leading craftsmen, Gustave Baumann, who is best known for his multicolor woodcuts.[9] The principal figure in the reredos is Christ the King; he is flanked by St. John and St. Paul, with rays symbolizing the Light of the World flowing though them. Movable side panels, which can be closed on solemn occasions such as Good Friday, depict Christ's message being received by the human races—white, black, American Indian, and Asian. The parish house was enlarged again, more significantly than before, in 1948; the new spaces provided room for parish offices and classrooms. A kitchen designed by Meem was built in 1950. When a new rectory was purchased in 1952, the old rectory built by Meem in 1939 was refurbished for use by the parish library. It too provided additional classrooms for the expanding church school.

Meem's last and most important work at Holy Faith involved the addition of a new chancel to the original church building. The problem at the church in Santa Fe was much the same as that at the cathedral in Albuquerque: Existing buildings proved inadequate in both cities, but the solutions were different. In Santa Fe the old church was not torn down but was retained as the nave, providing seating for the congregation, while a new chancel was constructed at its east end (liturgically east, that is; the actual direction is north). It was completed in 1954. Meem's design forms a perfect complement to the nineteenth-century building, and visitors often find it hard to believe that it was not part of the original scheme. It provides a fine setting for the Anthony–Baumann reredos. In the original building the reredos had been inserted in front of a large stained-glass window depicting the Good Shepherd (a reference to the fact that the parish had once borne that name), so that it stood in a cramped space and clashed in style with the Victorian glass. Meem retained this window but moved it to the Gospel side of the chancel and had three tall lancet windows made to stand above the altar. They are based on the Credo (the statement of belief) and designed with a number of small scenes in brilliant reds and blues. Here Meem chose the Judson Studios to do the work (this was a few years before he employed Connick Associates in Albuquerque). The cost, $5,000, was contributed by Meem as a memorial to his father.

In 1965 two more new windows, also by the Judson Studios, were placed on the side wall: a memorial to Mary Vilura Conkey depicts the Madonna and Child, and another shows St. Francis with some of the animals he so loved. Organ pipes would eventually project above the heads of choir members on the Epistle side of the chancel, although an electronic instrument was still in use during the 1950s. The vaulted wood ceiling, higher and more elaborate than that in the nave, is painted with designs in the same colors present in the new windows. A stone panel bearing a leaf design was placed under the organ loft. It had been carved in England of local limestone during the restoration of Lincoln Cathedral in the later eighteenth century and was given to Faith Bemis's father, Albert Farwell Bemis, in 1927. John Gaw Meem thought that it was an appropriate reminder of the church's centuries-old English traditions.

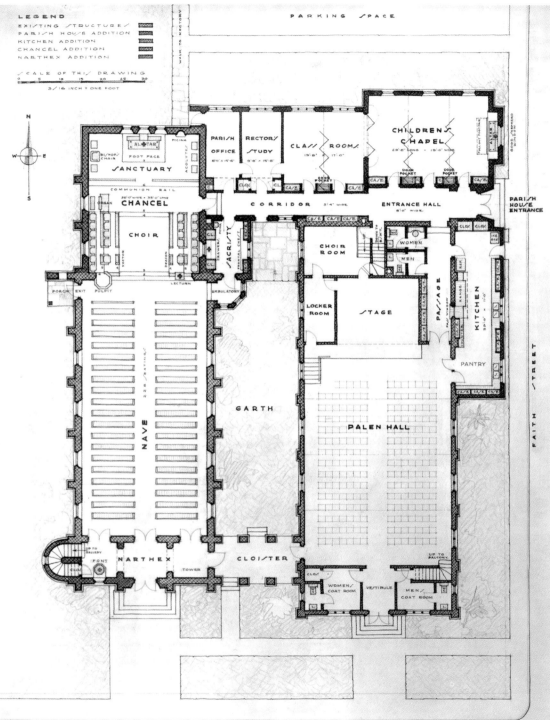

LEGEND
EXISTING STRUCTURE
PARISH HOUSE ADDITION
KITCHEN ADDITION
CHANCEL ADDITION
NARTHEX ADDITION

SCALE OF THIS DRAWING
0   5   10   15   20   25   30
3/16 INCH = ONE FOOT

PARKING SPACE

WALK TO RECTORY

N
W   E
S

ALTAR
BISHOP'S CHAIR   FOOT PACE   PICINA
SANCTUARY
ACOLYTE

PARISH OFFICE   RECTORY STUDY   CLASS ROOMS

CHILDRENS CHAPEL
29'6" LONG · 18'0" WIDE

ALTAR

GOOD SHEPHERD WINDOW

COMMUNION RAIL
ORGAN   CHANCEL   26'0" WIDE · 35'0" LONG

CHOIR

CL   CL   CA/E

PARISH HOUSE ENTRANCE

CLOS   CL   CA/E   DOOR POCKET   CA/E   DOOR POCKET   CL   DOOR POCKET   CA/E

CORRIDOR   5'4" WIDE

ENTRANCE HALL   5'0" WIDE

PORCH   EXIT   PULPIT   LECTERN   AMBULATORY

SACRISTY   FRONTAL CHEST

CA/E   CA/E   CA/E

CHOIR ROOM

CLOS   CLOS

ICE BOX

WOMEN
MEN

CLOS

REF.
RANGE

KITCHEN
30'0" × 15'0"

LOCKER ROOM

STAGE

PASSAGE

PANTRY

FAITH STREET

GARTH

NAVE
272 SEATING

PALEN HALL

UP TO GALLERY

UP TO BALCONY

NARTHEX   FONT   CLOS   TOWER   CLOISTER

WOMENS COAT ROOM   VESTIBULE   MENS COAT ROOM

CLOS   CA/E   CA/E   CA/E

EAST PALACE AVENUE

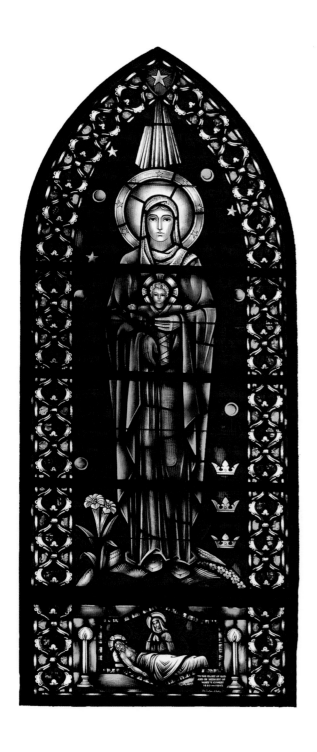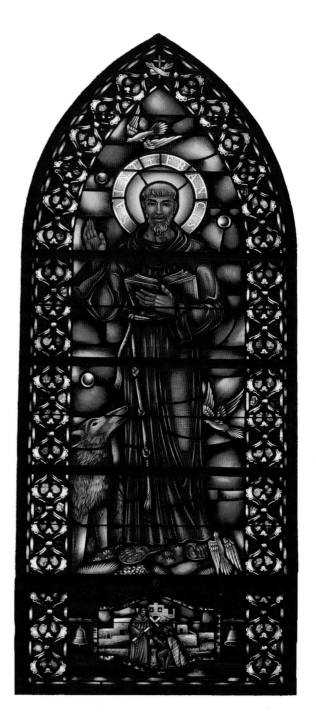

Meem's plans for Holy Faith also called for the addition of a narthex and balcony at the entrance to the church, opposite the new chancel. The narthex would incorporate the existing tower (as in Albuquerque) and provide shelter for those entering the building during inclement weather, and the balcony (reached by a staircase opposite the tower) would seat an additional forty people. A new baptismal font would be provided, symbolically located adjacent to the entrance to the church. Meem probably also had in mind designing a more impressive façade. Unfortunately funds for this work were not available in the 1950s, and it has never been undertaken. Proposals to add a bell to the tower also proved abortive. As late as 1975 Meem discussed plans for a new altar with the rector, Father Donald Campbell. Meem wanted a light-colored stone altar that could be supported by foundations provided when the chancel was constructed. The altar, he said, ought to have three carved stone panels on the front and a carved panel on each side. The central panel should have a symbol of Holy Faith and of the Eucharist, "as suggested by a drawing I made [earlier] for a wood altar," while the panel on the Gospel side should have symbols of hope and that on the Epistle side symbols of charity or love. The altar ought to be "constructed by the finest professional craftsmen in the U.S." and serve as a memorial to Miss Conkey. Meem thought that many parishioners would contribute to this endeavor, but he and Faith offered to pay the difference between the amount raised and the actual cost. The project, however, did not come to fruition. A simpler wood altar was eventually provided; as Meem recognized, "the argument against a stone altar and for a wood one is that the latter allows the priest the option of celebrating the Eucharist facing the congregation should he so desire."[10] The Holy Faith altar has, in fact, been moved forward for this reason.

After his retirement Meem was consulted about the construction of a new education building that would also contain office space, a lounge, a library, and a chapel. Named Conkey House in honor of Mary Vilura Conkey, who had left a legacy to the church, it was designed by Bradley P. Kidder, a former associate of Meem and a member of the parish. The original plans called for building a two-story structure, but funds were inadequate and the small Sunday School of the period did not seem to require upstairs spaces. The structure was modernized and the second floor finally added during a building campaign in the 1990s.

It is perhaps unfortunate that Meem was not able to reconstruct Holy Faith as fully as he did St. John's. The existing buildings, however, bear the unmistakable imprint of his personality, and the retention of the original nave bears testimony to his belief in historic preservation.

CHURCH OF THE HOLY FAITH. Windows depicting Madonna and Child (FACING PAGE, LEFT) and St. Francis (FACING PAGE, RIGHT).

DURING THESE YEARS Meem also worked for the Presbyterian churches in Taos and Albuquerque. During the 1940s the architect corresponded with J. P. Brandenburg, a banker and leading layman at the church in Taos. Brandenburg had been instrumental in securing the property adjacent to the park on the town's main street. Here an existing building needed to be replaced because it was too small and had no proper foundations. A scheme in 1941 merely to reroof it at a cost of $8,000–$10,000 was dropped in favor of plans for a new church. Brandenburg was clear that Meem was the only architect with whom he wished to work, because Meem knew more than anyone else about the Pueblo missions that should set the style for New Mexico churches. Meem agreed to prepare plans provided that Jack Brandenburg stood between him and members of the church who wished to direct the architect. As Brandenburg's widow Dorothy later put it, Meem did not want to have to deal with a committee of "little old gray-haired ladies." In particular, some parishioners wanted a bell tower, while Meem did not. A 1948 memorandum said that a seating capacity of 125 had been agreed on, but during the summer attendance ran as high as 150 or 160. Possibly a children's chapel adjacent to the main sanctuary might be arranged to provide additional seating. Five classrooms, an assembly room, and a kitchen were required. Specifications were completed in July 1951. The cost of the new building was estimated at $25,000. This seemed close, for the original contract with the builder, Dalton Montgomery, set a price of $27,773. In the end Montgomery's final bill was $40,218. Both he and Meem, however, made personal contributions to the work. Brandenburg, who was responsible for raising funds for the building, recalled that Meem said the only money due him was for his gas to drive to Taos and work on the project; Montgomery refused compensation for a number of extra expenses that arose during construction. "Dalton wanted to tell St. Peter at the Gates that when he was on the planet earth he built the First Presbyterian Church in Taos, New Mexico."[11]

Unlike the Episcopal churches in Albuquerque and Santa Fe, the building was indeed designed in the Southwest Pueblo Mission style that Meem had used at Cristo Rey. Its façade, which has battered buttresses, a balcony fronting a rectangular window, and a cross at the top, is similar to that in the Taylor Memorial Chapel, though somewhat simpler. Perhaps because of the question of erecting a tower, no bell is included in the building. Instead, the bell from the former church now sits on the ground near the entrance. The interior has a central aisle and at the east end a central altar. There is a large pulpit to the right and a small lectern to the left. A choir loft is at the west, above the entrance. All of the woodwork is unusually fine. The cross now mounted on the chancel wall is a later addition, designed by the son of the Taos architect and church

TAOS PRESBYTERIAN CHURCH.

TAOS PRESBYTERIAN CHURCH.

TAOS PRESBYTERIAN CHURCH. Original interior (LEFT) and present interior (BELOW).

TAOS PRESBYTERIAN CHURCH. Balcony.

elder Cameron Mactavish; the younger Mactavish practices architecture in Philadelphia. Bainbridge Bunting regarded the church as one of Meem's successful, for despite its relatively small size its plain form produces a "truly monumental effect." It is hard to disagree with that judgment.[12]

IN THE SPRING OF 1948 Meem received a letter from C. C. Broome, a businessman in Albuquerque, saying that a new Presbyterian church had been organized "in the Heights here in Albuquerque" (actually, at Carlisle and Silver streets), in the Nob Hill area east of the university campus. The site was indeed a splendid one, near the Tijeras Arroyo and rising above the flat lands that characterized most of the city. It adjoined a residential area that was one of Albuquerque's most desirable new communities. Broome wrote that "our members are interested in the Territorial Colonial type of building, and it has been pointed out that your experience in this type of building is

IMMANUEL PRESBYTERIAN CHURCH, ALBUQUERQUE.
Study (LEFT) and plan (BELOW).

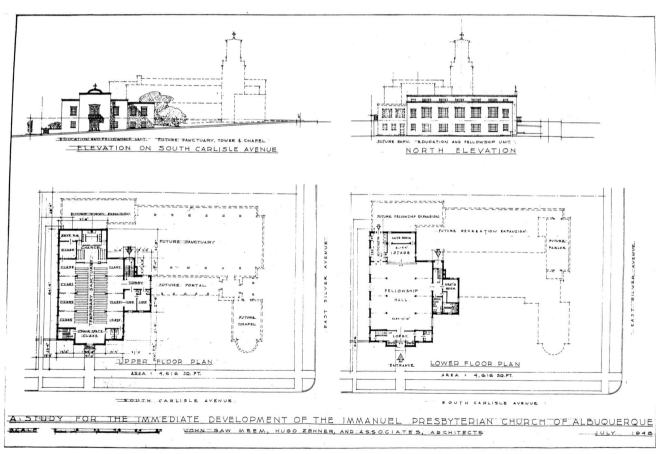

ELEVATION ON SOUTH CARLISLE AVENUE

NORTH ELEVATION

UPPER FLOOR PLAN
AREA = 4,616 SQ. FT.

LOWER FLOOR PLAN
AREA = 4,616 SQ. FT.

SOUTH CARLISLE AVENUE

SOUTH CARLISLE AVENUE

A STUDY FOR THE IMMEDIATE DEVELOPMENT OF THE IMMANUEL PRESBYTERIAN CHURCH OF ALBUQUERQUE
SCALE — JOHN GAW MEEM, HUGO ZEHNER, AND ASSOCIATES, ARCHITECTS — JULY, 1948

IMMANUEL PRESBYTERIAN CHURCH. Original entrance (LEFT) and present exterior (BELOW).

**IMMANUEL PRESBYTERIAN
CHURCH.** Chapel (original sanctuary).

**IMMANUEL PRESBYTERIAN
CHURCH.** Tower.

such that we would like to discuss the possibilities of you undertaking the commission."[13] A meeting took place on May 4 at Broome's furniture store, and plans were immediately undertaken. It was agreed that the church should be built in several phases, but early drawings from Meem's office show that he conceived the entire structure as finally built almost from the beginning, even though detailed plans were drawn only for the first phase. According to Meem's memorandum the original unit could include no more than 7,000 square feet because "$65,000 to $70,000 is the maximum they dare try to raise on [their] first drive," and $10 a square foot was a reasonable cost estimate. This building would eventually house the educational plant rather than the sanctuary, with a fellowship room and kitchen on the ground floor and the Sunday school auditorium above. This auditorium would serve as a temporary sanctuary seating 400 people; here Meem would "try to get [a] churchly atmosphere in spite of low ceilings and many windows."[14]

Meem's plans were unanimously approved by the congregation. Immanuel member Fred Mossman was chosen as the building contractor, and ground was broken in June 1949. Construction involved the use of large commercial bricks and stucco, not the handmade mud bricks used at Acoma and Cristo Rey, with steel girders supporting the roof. The first building was completed in less than a year. It was indeed in the Territorial Revival style, with a flat roof and walls capped by a red brick coping, rather than the curved adobe of the Pueblo churches or Cristo Rey. The main entrance, on the west side, consisted of double doors with triple lights above wood panels. The doors were surmounted by a transom and flanked by Doric wood pilasters. An entablature with dentils rested on top of the pilasters, and a small balcony rested on the entablature. A low curved parapet with an iron cross was centered on the top of the building above the doors. Large recessed steel windows lit the fellowship hall and the classrooms above, and octagonal clerestory windows helped contribute the "churchly atmosphere" of the sanctuary. All of these were filled with clear glass. The exterior was cream-colored stucco with a red brick coping and white window surrounds.

In a letter inviting Meem to the dedication of the building, Broome wrote, "Your generous and kind assistance has made it possible for us to complete the educational unit of our church. After you have inspected this fine building, I believe you will be glad you had a part in its realization." Dedicated on April 23, 1950, the building and all its furnishings had cost $125,000. The new church had 277 members. The Rev. J. Elbert Nash was the senior pastor, and the Rev. J. Denton Simms was his associate. Simms would serve at Immanuel for twenty-eight years; when the original sanctuary became a chapel, it was named in his honor.

The second unit was added to the east side, the back of the original building. A preliminary study had proposed two bowling lanes, but they were eliminated in the final plans. Instead, the addition provided more classrooms, a small stage, and a multipurpose recreational area. It was completed in 1951.

Ground was broken for the third and last unit in October of 1954. Fred Mossman again served as contractor. Built on the south side of the original unit, the addition included the present sanctuary, the third story, and the bell tower. It also included the 10-foot-wide portal along the west side of the building. Six pairs of square Doric columns support the plain architrave, frieze, and cornice above the portal. Broad curves between the arches are repeated on the parapet above the entrance to the first unit. A series of broad steps leads up to an entrance on the north end of the portal, and a balustrade encloses the west side of the portal south of the steps. The windows on the ground floor are like those on that of the original unit. Wood surrounds, cornices, and sills on the second- and third-story windows repeat the classical features of those on the second story of the original building. A large square tower rises above all the other building blocks and supports a wood balustrade around a low platform; a wooden bell tower with a metal cross at its top rests on this platform. The open tower set the style for what was to become almost a signature for Meem's secular architecture; it is similar,

IMMANUEL PRESBYTERIAN CHURCH.
Sanctuary (ABOVE) and altar and carved cross (FACING PAGE).

for instance, to the towers he designed for St. Francis Cathedral School and the administration building of St. John's College. Wherever such a tower is used, it can be seen from a distance, and it dominates the approach to the building it crowns.

The new sanctuary accommodates 576 people on the main floor and another 125 in the balcony. It displays several architectural elements that are characteristic of Meem's work. The proportions of the relatively long narrow nave are reminiscent of the mission churches that he loved. Clear light originally poured in through the octagonal clerestory windows as well as through the large rectangular windows on the east side of the sanctuary. (Stained glass was inserted into the clerestory windows in the 1970s; recent-

ly there has been talk of removing it.) Light also enters through hidden windows above the chancel—again, a feature of such churches as Acoma and Cristo Rey. Large star-shaped light fixtures, individually crafted of punched tin, and smaller recessed fixtures provide additional illumination. Seating is arranged between a central and two peripheral aisles. The dark pews contrast with the warm rosy shades of the walls and the creamy color of the paneling; the ceiling is a soft cerulean blue. The colors, of course, were chosen by Meem. The choir and chancel railings, elders' seats, pulpit, lectern, Communion table, and other furnishings were designed by Meem and built by Immanuel member George Weidner. For a time it was thought that the woodwork would be pine, because it was relatively inexpensive, but in the end more attractive walnut was used.

Dedicated on November 28, 1956, the last addition was completed at a cost of $355,246. Carillonic bells and a pipe organ were installed as part of the third unit. The chancel cross, a dominant feature that was designed by Meem and carved by Weidner, was added a few years later. According to Mr. Weidner,

> Each of the panels of the cross was built as a separate unit in accordance with the architect's drawings . . . from a two-inch thick walnut wood slab two feet square. Except for the outline and cut-outs of each medallion, the relief carving was done with a few carving tools and a wood mallet. Working a few hours a day, it required about three months to make and install the panels.

Four of the panels represent the apostles Matthew, Mark, Luke, and John as winged creatures. Each is holding an open Bible imprinted with an alpha and omega; as the first and last letters of the Greek alphabet, they symbolize the beginning and the end of Creation. The lily shown at the bottom of the cross appears to wither and die but returns to blossom every spring—a symbol of Christ's resurrection and immortality.

Immanuel Presbyterian remains one of Meem's most important churches. It is one of the largest, and it is virtually unchanged since his time. It is the principal church Meem designed in the Territorial style. Although this style was originally chosen at the request of the church members who sought his services, it is also a style very characteristic of Meem and appears in many of his houses and secular buildings.

TWO SIMILAR BUILDINGS designed by Meem in the 1940s represent the continuation of the Pueblo Adobe style used in Taos. Correspondence relating to St. James's Episcopal Church in Clovis began in 1941, while the Rt. Rev. Frederick B. Bartlett was

bishop in charge of the church, although ground was not broken until May 1949. Here an existing building, put up in 1909, was clearly inadequate. It was taken down and a new church, parish house, and rectory were planned as one unit. Meem's façade displays large battered buttresses that project beyond the side walls. A double door is surmounted by a rectangular window and a balcony, above which is a stepped bell tower and cross. The thick walls are built of handmade sun-dried adobes, as at Cristo Rey. They support heavy yellow pine *vigas* that are 35 feet long. The bricks were made locally, but the beams were trucked in from Santa Fe. A solid adobe altar with an altar stone

**ST. JAMES'S EPISCOPAL
CHURCH.**

ST. JAMES'S EPISCOPAL CHURCH.
Original interior (LEFT) and present interior (BELOW).

embedded in its mensa rests directly upon the solid earth. The rectangular windows hold their original plain opaque glass rather than figurative stained glass. The building seats just over a hundred. The parish house lies to the right of the main building, behind the sanctuary.

The church was consecrated by Bishop Stoney on September 12, 1950. It received more publicity than most of Meem's churches: Photographs of it appeared on the front cover of *The Southwest Churchman* in November 1949 and *The Living Church* on October 15, 1950, and the rector, the Rev. Ross Calvin, described it in an article titled "Built in the Tradition of the Pharaohs," printed in the journal *Forth*. (A well-known writer, Calvin had published a book, *The Sky Determines*, and other studies of the Southwest.) When the work was complete, Meem wrote Calvin, "We have never had a client that was more appreciative than you and we deeply appreciate it."[15] The building was restored about 1990; all in all, it it is a little gem, one of Meem's most beautiful churches.[16]

In 1946 Pastor Walter Geihsler wrote Meem regarding the design of a new building for Immanuel Lutheran Church on Barcelona Road in southern Santa Fe. "The talk among our people has been decidedly in favor of the Indian Pueblo style with vigas, etc."; this was preferred over the Territorial style. The church was to seat about a hundred people and was to have a basement housing an assembly room. Not unusually, the pastor hoped that Meem would be able to keep the cost as low as possible.[17]

The building was completed in 1948. As usual, Meem's fee was 6 percent of the total cost, which included his supervision as well as plans and specifications. The church has remarkable similarities to the structure in Clovis, though the entrance façade is simpler, without a balcony. There is a small pediment intended to house a bell, although one was not initially installed. Battered buttresses are omitted, and a side view shows the stairwell necessary for use of the basement. The interior has no balcony or choir loft; a central aisle leads to the railed altar with a large pulpit to its right and a small lectern to the left. Originally a curtain hung behind the altar, but this has been replaced by a more modern cross. *Vigas* supported by carved corbels hold up the roof, as the church members had wished. The chandeliers chosen by Meem remain. Meem's original drawing shows a pastor's office attached to the right rear of the church, but it was actually built to the left. The rectangular windows originally held clear glass; the present stained glass is a later addition. Classrooms were added in 1964, and the sanctuary was extended toward the north in 1989, but the existing altar and other fittings were retained, and Meem's style was followed so scrupulously that the observer is not aware of the change.

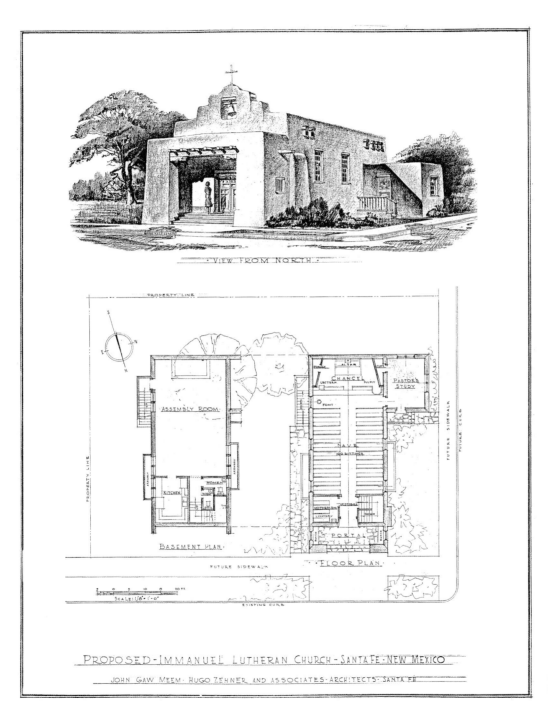

·VIEW·FROM·NORTH·

ASSEMBLY·ROOM·

KITCHEN

BASEMENT·PLAN·

SCALE: 1/8"=1'-0"

CHANCEL

PASTOR'S STUDY

NAVE

PORTAL

·FLOOR·PLAN·

PROPOSED·IMMANUEL·LUTHERAN·CHURCH·SANTA FE·NEW MEXICO

JOHN GAW MEEM · HUGO ZEHNER AND ASSOCIATES · ARCHITECTS · SANTA FE

**IMMANUEL
LUTHERAN CHURCH.**
Plan.

IMMANUEL LUTHERAN CHURCH, SANTA FE.

IMMANUEL LUTHERAN CHURCH. Light fixture (RIGHT) and interior (BELOW).

LESSER WORK OF THE 1940S involved churches in Las Vegas and Roswell. In 1947 the Rev. Frank W. Duggan employed Meem to redesign the chancel area of the First Presbyterian Church of Las Vegas—this was, of course, the city in New Mexico, not Nevada, which had been an important center earlier than Santa Fe because of the coming of the railroad there. A drawing from Meem's office reveals an interior that seems surprisingly high-church for the Presbyterians: There is a rood loft with a cross, a central altar with the lectern to the left and the pulpit to the right, and a divided choir seated on two sides. Simple stained-glass windows were installed and a kitchen and second-floor classroom were provided. Correspondence with the Reuter organ company survives. As minutes of a church meeting noted, "the church will have one of the most worshipful and attractive sanctuaries in the State."[18]

Additions to St. Paul's Episcopal Church in Las Vegas were undertaken in 1949. The church had been established as a mission in 1879, and the cornerstone for the present building was laid in 1886. Facing stone came from the old courthouse building, which had been demolished. The church was designated as the home church of the first resident Episcopal bishop of the New Mexico–Arizona territory, George K. Dunlop. Here, as at Holy Faith in Santa Fe, a new chancel was added to an existing historic building. Once again Meem had three lancet windows installed above the altar; in this case they were made by the D'Ascenzo Studios of Philadelphia, who had worked at the National Cathedral in Washington, D. C. The Reuter company was consulted about the organ chamber. Meem's additions cost about $14,250.[19]

In addition, Meem designed a parsonage for the First Methodist Church of Las Vegas in 1948. "It is a very simple house," he commented, "but I believe it will be good looking."[20]

St. Andrew's Church in Roswell was one of the earliest missions of the Episcopal Church in New Mexico. It had been founded in 1894, and its first building was completed in 1900. A parish house was added in 1925 and some classrooms in 1939, while the Rt. Rev. Frederick B. Howden was bishop of the Missionary District of New Mexico and Texas, west of the Pecos. Four years later the bishop's son, Frederick B. Howden Jr., came to Roswell as rector of St. Andrew's. Always known as Ted, the younger Howden was thought of as being an "easy mixer" with all sorts of people, though by nature reserved and taciturn; he was a leader of the Boy Scouts and worked as an assistant chaplain at the New Mexico Military Institute in Roswell. Shortly after the outbreak of World War II, he volunteered to serve as a military chaplain. These duties took him to the Philippines, and after the defeat of American troops by the Japanese, he was taken prisoner and became part of the infamous Bataan "death march." Here he died;

ST. PAUL'S EPISCOPAL
CHURCH, LAS VEGAS.

**ST. PAUL'S EPISCOPAL
CHURCH.** Sanctuary (ABOVE),
altar (RIGHT), and window above
altar (FACING PAGE).

it was said that he starved to death, having given his meager rations to other deprived men.

In 1946 leaders of the church in Roswell determined that their building should be rebuilt and enlarged as a memorial to Ted Howden. The following summer they wrote to Meem, asking him to serve as architect, and in November 1947 he went to Roswell to meet with the building committee. Meem wrote:

> I inspected the present church with them. It is quite old fashioned, having been built around 1900 or even earlier, but has considerable charm on account of its unassuming simplicity. . . . After a great deal of discussion, it was agreed that the smart thing to do would be to build the new church with an east and west axis. The new church should have a seating capacity of about 200 and the preliminary plans should be comprehensive enough to include the total future development, including the expansion of the Sunday School unit.

Because of difficulties in fund-raising, construction did not begin until 1950, when Bishop Stoney broke ground on March 12. Work was completed late in 1951. Since it was hoped that the cost would not exceed $50,000 (in the end, it ran to about $80,000), Meem retained most of the existing building, adding a new aisle and a tower, which was eventually to be capped by a spire, even if that was initially too expensive. Like many of the Episcopal churches, St. Andrew's was designed in the Gothic style, but in an effort at cost containment Meem used stucco rather than stone for the exterior. There are low stone courses at the bottom of the walls, and an attractive English-style entrance porch has half-timbered detailing.[21]

BOTH THE NUMBER and the beauty of the church designs that flowed from Meem's office during the 1940s are astonishing. He demonstrated an ability to work happily and sympathetically in at least three different idioms, the Adobe or Pueblo Mission style employed most often for smaller buildings like the Presbyterian church in Taos or the Lutheran church in Santa Fe; the English Gothic style favored by Episcopal churches in Albuquerque and Santa Fe; and the Territorial style requested at Immanuel Presbyterian Church. Careful engineering as well as elegant design, together with a remarkable attention to detail, characterize all these buildings. It is fortunate that most of them are lovingly cared for and remain essentially unchanged, so that present-day visitors can appreciate Meem's genius.

ST. ANDREW'S CHURCH, ROSWELL. Drawing for addition.

ST. ANDREW'S CHURCH.
Exterior (ABOVE AND FACING
PAGE, TOP) and interior (FACING
PAGE, BOTTOM).

SACRED HEART CATHOLIC CATHEDRAL, GALLUP. Drawing.

THREE

THE LAST DECADE, 1952–1960

THE LAST TEN YEARS of Meem's professional career, the decade of the 1950s, saw the design of two of his most important works, Sacred Heart Catholic Cathedral in Gallup, New Mexico, and the Good Shepherd (Episcopal) Mission in Fort Defiance, Arizona. Several smaller commissions were executed during these years as well.

As early as 1943 Meem's office had been contacted about the cathedral in Gallup. On May 1 Fr. Pax R. Schicker had written to Meem's associate, Hugo Zehner, asking for "a front elevation of a simple but imposing cathedral structure embodying some type of architecture in keeping with this Navajo city" west of Santa Fe, near the border between New Mexico and Arizona. A few days later Schicker sent details of the proposed building site, and on May 17 Meem wrote Schicker that he was sending a plan and perspective drawing for consideration by the bishop, Msgr. Bernard T. Espelage.[1] The architect described his proposed building in some detail:

> The building we have suggested can be built of brick, adobe, or stone, and has been shown with over-hanging roof which eliminates parapet walls. This is a type of construction which gives maximum protection and yet retains many of the features of the local architecture. If you prefer a straight Spanish-Pueblo type of structure, the scheme suggested can easily be converted to this type of architecture. . . . The scheme we have in mind calls for a rather high central nave, well lighted from clear-story windows, spanned with wooden trusses occurring

SACRED HEART CATHOLIC CATHEDRAL.

**SACRED HEART
CATHOLIC CATHEDRAL.**
Model (LEFT) and interior
(BELOW).

over the large piers; purling in turn being either round or square section timbers bearing on the trusses, and showing the actual construction. The ceiling can be decorated to produce a very nice effect. The Sanctuary has been made approximately the same size as the St. Francis Cathedral here, and should give ample room for normal usage and for larger rituals.

It would seat 725 persons.

Schicker responded that he and Bishop Espelage were pleased with the designs, and he sent details of the site proposed for construction. But funds were not available, and in any case it would be impossible to begin building until after the end of the war.

Discussions were underway again early in 1946, and Meem's memorandum of a meeting held January 24 suggests that there was, in fact, no agreement about the architectural conception:

> As to style, they would prefer Gothic, but will be guided by our recommendations. They are not impressed with the necessity for any local type of architecture in Gallup, reflecting the region [perhaps because they had been born elsewhere]. The local stone is not beautiful. They suggested terra cotta finish in shiny slabs like the Telephone Building in Albuquerque, but I think we can talk them out of that.

They hoped that the cathedral could be built for $150,000, "as it would be difficult to carry a greater debt than that."

Meem agreed to build in brick rather than stone or adobe, and he was willing to consider brick from a local plant in Gallup. In 1947 he prepared a model of his scheme, so that the proposed building might be viewed from different perspectives, and he developed a set of plans including drawings of light fixtures. It was agreed that the cathedral would cost about $350,000 and that Meem's fee would be 6 percent. But the money was still not there, and the building site turned out to be smaller than originally believed. In April 1949 Meem wrote Espelage, wondering "if we shouldn't start all over again and plan a smaller church which you could build in the near future, although I can't help hoping with all my heart that the Cathedral as we have planned it will be built." Instead of the Reuter organ recommended by the organist of the Episcopal cathedral in Albuquerque, Joseph W. Grant, it was agreed to "figure on a Hammond temporarily."

Construction finally began in 1953. In March Meem revised the plans in order to bring costs within the bishop's new limit of $375,000. There is a fine drawing of the modified design, probably executed by Edward Holien. The clerestory windows have been deleted and the roof lowered in order to save money, although the cathedral still

SACRED HEART CATHOLIC CATHEDRAL. Chapel.

conveys the impression of a lofty building. Fittings were commissioned, with an emphasis on quality rather than economy. These included a stone altar made by the Cold Spring Granite Company of Minnesota as well as a crucifix for the main altar, stone statues for the side altars, and ceramic Stations of the Cross provided by M. Loriaux of the Santa Fe Studios of Church Art. The crucifix was to be carved of lindenwood by Vigilio Prugger and waxed without color, except for the gold-leaf loin cloth; it was to be 13 feet high and 9 feet wide and to cost $1,980. Meem's friend Eugenie Shonnard would carve designs on the stone above the main entrance. "She is an excellent sculptress and by having her do this work you will be assured of a first class job," he wrote.[2]

(FOLLOWING PAGES)
SACRED HEART CATHOLIC CATHEDRAL. Window honoring missionary Fray Juan Ramirez (LEFT) and window honoring the builder of Sacred Heart Catholic Cathedral (RIGHT).

94

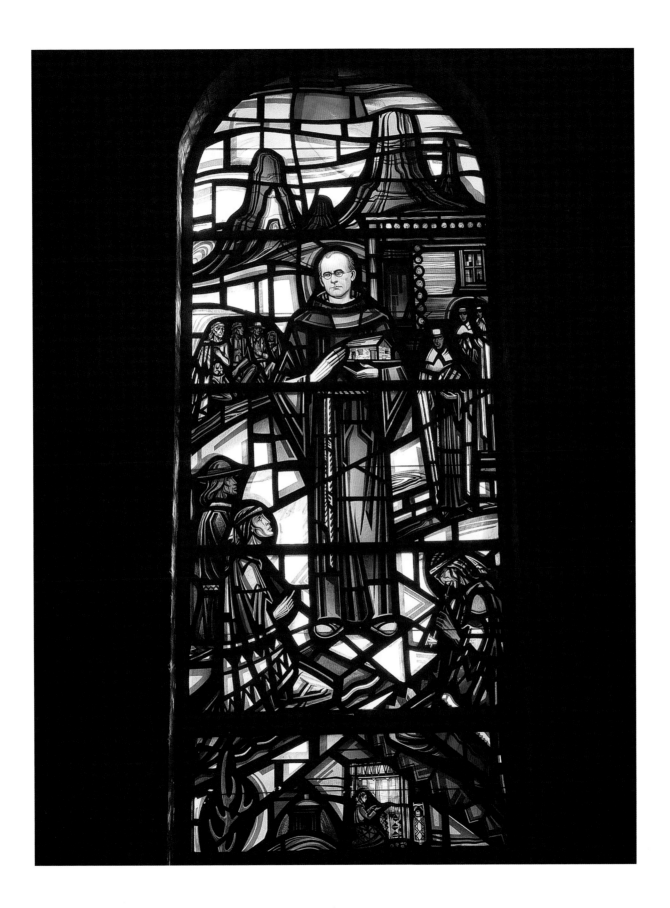

The cathedral was dedicated on Sunday afternoon, November 28, 1954. Meem's wife and daughter, Faith and Nancy, were with him at the service, but only John was invited to attend the all-male banquet that followed.

Sacred Heart in Gallup is not one of Meem's best known works, perhaps because it is not in Santa Fe and perhaps because it is not in the Santa Fe style. But it is surely one of his finest buildings, elegantly designed and carefully executed. Although it may not be as grand as he originally hoped, its height and spaciousness strike the viewer immediately. The stained glass, installed when funds became available, floods the interior with brilliantly colored light. The red brick, if not the most sophisticated building material, was laid with great attention to detail, especially in the curving arches. The architectural style seems Meem's own: It is not based on Pueblo churches (like Cristo Rey) or Territorial buildings (like Immanuel Presbyterian) or English Gothic (like St. John's Cathedral or Holy Faith). If anything, its round arches make it appear Romanesque. (There is a tradition in Gallup that Bishop Espelage believed Romanesque to be the only proper ecclesiastical style and urged Meem to adopt it.) A portal edges the right-hand side of the church and helps tie it to a regional tradition. The cathedral complex includes offices and a clergy residence designed by Meem as well as a family center built later; standing on a slight hill, it dominates its section of the city, above the busy railroad and freeway below.

LIKE THE CATHEDRAL IN GALLUP, the Alumni Chapel on the campus of the University of New Mexico had been under discussion since the 1940s. It was in 1944, shortly before the end of the Second World War, that the construction of a chapel honoring alumni who had lost their lives in the war was proposed. By 1948 a fund drive had begun and by 1953 $40,000 had been contributed. It was natural for Meem to be involved because he was the university architect, responsible for all its buildings. Plans were drawn in 1954 but the estimated cost, $85,000, exceeded the amount available at that time ($75,000), so Meem was asked to eliminate the proposed *retablos* and other interior fittings. A contract with the builders Bradbury and Stamm was not signed until 1960. The final cost was $160,000.

The façade of the chapel is very much like that of the Episcopal church in Clovis, with battered buttresses, a balcony, and a turret, in this case housing two bells. Landscaping was designed by Meem's associate Edward Holien, and a reredos, based on sketches made earlier by Meem, was carved by the university's art professor, John Tatschl, and painted by John M. Gonzales of Las Vegas. The panels include Christian symbolism, but because the chapel is available to all alumni, they were installed in such

A WAR MEMORIAL CHAPEL

FOR THE UNIVERSITY ALUMNI ASSOCIATION OF THE UNIVERSITY OF NEW MEXICO

JOHN GAW MEEM, HUGO ZEHNER, AND ASSOCIATES, ARCHITECTS

WAR MEMORIAL CHAPEL,
UNIVERSITY OF NEW
MEXICO.

WAR MEMORIAL CHAPEL.
Exterior (FACING PAGE) and
interior (RIGHT).

a way that they could be removed when the building was used for Jewish or other non-Christian memorial services or weddings. Now they are simply covered with a flag or fabric hanging when desired. Carved panels list the names of the fallen alumni. The chapel was not dedicated until February 18, 1962.[3]

In 1952 Meem undertook the remodeling of Grace Episcopal Church in Carlsbad. Here there was a fine historic building, erected in 1890 and made of stone in the Gothic style. But it seated only seventy-two, and the present congregation was twice that size. Meem's solution was a design similar to the one he created for Holy Faith in Santa Fe: He retained the existing structure as the nave and added a new chancel, sanctuary, sacristy, and priest's study. A large tower dominates exterior views of the building. The result is beautiful; the church appears unified, and only a person familiar with its history would realize that it did not date from a single time.[4]

About 1955, the Rev. Al Tarbell, who had been given responsibility for starting a new Episcopal mission on the northeast side of Albuquerque, contacted Meem to request plans for a building. Sketches and specifications were submitted, and construction was undertaken in 1957. As often happened with new missions, the church was to be built in two stages, the first of which would provide a parish house to be used also as a sanctuary until the entire scheme was realized. Several years later, in 1961, plans for an addition were accepted. Later the parish merged with another Episcopal church, St. Aidan's, and assumed the new name of St. Mary's. They then sold their building, located at the intersection of Claremont and Wyoming, to the Grant Chapel African Methodist Episcopal Church. The building is still in use, and the church flourishes as one of the earliest African-American congregations in Albuquerque.[5]

Another project of the 1950s involved St. Andrew's Episcopal Church in Las Cruces. Here a mission had been founded in 1911 by Bishop John Mills Kendrick. Its earliest building, a small chapel, was erected in 1913 to serve Episcopalians who earlier had been forced to travel to the older church in Mesilla, which dated from 1870. The Kendrick chapel, a Gothic brick structure with a small bell tower, still exists and is used for weddings and other small services. A parish house built of adobe had been added in 1935, but as Meem later noted, had "given nothing but trouble ever since." Meem was employed in 1954 to remodel the parish house and add a new kitchen at a cost estimated at $50,000. In the end the total expenses were just over $70,000.

A large church and colonnade, also designed by Meem, were added between 1960 and 1962, and sculpture by Eugenie Shonnard was included. Some of these designs involved the use of what was called "Keenstone," a form of concrete that Shonnard had developed. Her work may be seen in the parish hall windows and in the capitals and bases of the columns in front of the building. A beautiful drawing from Meem's office, reproduced in a fund-raising brochure, shows a building in the Territorial style, verging on baroque. The principal pedimented entrance has a balconied window above an exceptionally elaborate surround, again executed by Shonnard in Keenstone. The bell tower, attached but designed as a separate element, provides space for not one but three bells, hung one above another, and a five-bay portal links the church with an auditorium. Stained-glass windows, like some of the work at the Alumni Chapel, were designed by John Tatschl of the university.[6]

Meem was also involved in the construction of a new building on the Old Pecos Trail for the First Baptist Church of Santa Fe, which had been founded in 1917. Since

GRACE EPISCOPAL CHURCH, CARLSBAD.

GRACE EPISCOPAL CHURCH.
Addition (ABOVE) and interior (RIGHT).

ST. ANDREW'S EPISCOPAL CHURCH, LAS CRUCES. Exterior (ABOVE) and interior (LEFT).

ST. ANDREW'S EPISCOPAL CHURCH. Study.

1921 church members had been worshiping in a building at the corner of Manhattan Avenue and Don Gaspar, but this structure had become inadequate and was eventually sold and demolished. The new church was erected on a large plot of land, nearly ten acres, purchased in 1955. Construction began in 1959 and the church was dedicated in December 1960. The design work was actually undertaken by William R. Buckley of Meem's office, but Meem offered advice and the structure is clearly in his Pueblo Mission style, including a tower reminiscent of that at Cristo Rey. The building, which cost $292,000, was dedicated in December 1960.[7]

ONE OF MEEM'S LAST COMMISSIONS, and one of his most interesting ones, involved the Good Shepherd Mission in Fort Defiance, Arizona. Fort Defiance was an important center of missionary work with the Navajo, many of whom had been turned out of their native lands in 1864 and made to join a forced march or "long walk" to Fort Sumner, north of Roswell and three hundred miles away from their homes. Those who survived were allowed to return to a Navajo reservation in 1868. Fort Defiance, near Gallup in New Mexico and Window Rock in Arizona, was established as the Navajo Agency's center for administration and distribution of goods. It also became an important trading center.[8]

The Episcopal Church almost immediately took an interest in providing assistance for the Native Americans. Its Good Shepherd Mission first built a small hospital on the reservation, followed by a specialized eye clinic, which was needed because eye infections were chronic among this population. Then there was a boarding school and dormitories for the schoolchildren; the housing facilities continued to function even after public schools were opened. Late in the 1940s Arthur Kinsolving, Bishop of Arizona, became interested in replacing the old chapel. Arthur was a cousin of Meem's friend Charles Kinsolving, rector of Holy Faith in Santa Fe and soon to become bishop of the Rio Grande. Perhaps because of this connection, Arthur wrote Meem on December 31, 1949, explaining that since only the exterior of the church had been completed, it should be demolished and replaced by a fine new building. He asked Meem to undertake the project. Agreeing to do so, Meem prepared plans for a large chapel and some additional buildings, including a residence for the missionary priest. A grant of nearly $4,000 was given by the Episcopal Church Foundation of Arizona and very generous additional funding was provided by Arthur Vining Davis.[9]

The story of Davis's involvement is fascinating. The son of a Congregational minister in Roxbury, Massachusetts, he had gone to Pittsburgh to work with Charles Martin Hall in attempting to find a cheaper way to make aluminum. Their efforts were suc-

**GOOD SHEPHERD MISSION,
FORT DEFIANCE, ARIZONA.**
Exterior (ABOVE) and original mission (RIGHT); the church is the building on the left.

**GOOD SHEPHERD
MISSION.** Interior (ABOVE)
and crucifix (RIGHT).

**THE REV. DAVIS
GIVEN,** missionary to
Fort Defiance; photo
taken about 1954.

cessful and, with financial backing from the Mellon family and others, they established the Aluminum Company of America. Arthur Vining Davis became the founding president of Alcoa and, in time, a notable philanthropist; the foundation that bears his name still supports many projects, including public television programming.[10]

Davis himself had no special interest in Native Americans but came to assist them because of the work of his step-grandson, Davis Given. Because the aluminum magnate had no children of his own, he regarded Given and his sister as virtually his own offspring. Davis Given became interested in the Navajo people because of a youthful experience in New Mexico. His college roommate had attended the Los Alamos Ranch School before it was closed to make way for the national laboratories that developed the atomic bomb.[11] Davis Given wrote:

I first went to the Southwest in the summer of 1941 because he was a counselor at the summer camp run by his school. I went again the summer of 1942 (after our graduation from Yale) for a pack-trip to the Jemez mountains with my roommate and another Los Alamos friend of his—with school horses, pack horses, and a school wrangler—before we both went into military service for the war. The two Los Alamos students often made trips to the Navajo Reservation. That was my introduction. The summer after I got out of the service I went back to Santa Fe and again to Los Pinos (up the Pecos), and both summers as a seminary student (at General Theological), 1947 and 1948, I went to Good Shepherd on a program for seminarians helping with Vacation Bible Schools. As a deacon, released by the Bishop of Long Island, I went to work at Good Shepherd and was ordained a priest in the old chapel in November 1949 by Bishop Kinsolving.[12]

Father Given remained at Good Shepherd until 1963. He worked very closely with Meem in developing the building project there. In 1952 Meem came to Fort Defiance to meet with Given and Arthur Vining Davis. Plans were drawn, and the church building was completed in 1954. The architect's involvement was amazingly comprehensive, considering that his office lay hundreds of miles away. In addition to designing the church, he planned an imposing residence for Davis Given. This design proved to be

GOOD SHEPHERD MISSION.
Aluminum window grills.

GOOD SHEPHERD MISSION.
Aluminum window grills.

GOOD SHEPHERD MISSION.
Window grills seen from inside
church.

GOOD SHEPHERD MISSION.
Baptistry (ABOVE) and Aluminum
baptismal font (RIGHT).

GOOD SHEPHERD MISSION. Tower.

costly and controversial. It was a large building—4,500 square feet—and contained a guest suite, maid's room, library, and offices as well as the usual living quarters. Given's father, William B. Given Jr., who was president of the American Brake Shoe Company in New York, was concerned about the expense; he wrote Meem that funds were not unlimited. Arthur Vining Davis, too, at one time was unhappy about the cost, which turned out to be about $60,000—a substantial amount in the 1950s. Meem himself admitted that "this is an expensive house, even if it were not being built in a remote place." The Lembke Company of Albuquerque had been chosen to do the work. Problems with water and electrical supply, with roads and grading, and with the septic system continued for years, repeatedly requiring Meem's attention and attempts at reconciliation.

"Mr. Meem was responsible for every detail," Given later wrote, and he made a number of personal gifts to the chapel. These included Mexican tin hymn boards and silver candlesticks made by the Navajo artist Kenneth Begay. Given added that Meem

> arranged for Carl Larsson (a distinguished Santa Fe artist in silver, glass and plainting) to make the nine-foot hanging cross over the main altar with its central Agnus Dei and terminals of the four Evangelists in silver with turquoise ceramic "backgrounds" by Eugenie Shonnard, a Santa Fe artist. He designed the aluminum "grills" for the clear glass windows, with plant motifs from Navajo sandpaintings. Navajo stone masons did all the work with local pink sandstone. An "appropriate touch"—considering A. V. Davis's involvement with the Aluminum Company of America—were aluminum altar railings, the cover and bowl for the baptismal font, the window grills and the "bell turret" of the church tower, and plaques for the original chapel and its donor and for a memorial for my grandmother.[13]

Even more than the cathedral at Gallup, the church at Fort Defiance is an expression of Meem's own design rather than an exercise in recapturing an older style. Its most remarkable feature is, of course, the use of aluminum, something unique to this building as well as a reminder of the involvement of Arthur Vining Davis. As Fr. Given said, fine aluminum grills or screens add interest to the windows, which are otherwise plain large rectangles of clear glass, except for a few small panels of stained glass rescued from the old church and reused in the aisles and baptistry. The aluminum bell tower is the dominant feature of the exterior and can be seen from a distance, leading the visitor to the church itself. The baptismal font has an aluminum bowl and cover.[14] A dominant feature of the interior is the crucifix that hangs above the altar. When it was first installed in September 1954, Given wrote Meem, wondering, "Is the hanging cross too large, at 9' or more in length? Are the silver rosettes needed? Would the medallions at the center and extremities be enough?"[15] The original altar had to be reworked, but in June 1955 Given sent Meem word that it was back. "The top is now a piece of Texas limestone painted pink. The supports are the original stones, I think, painted pink to match the top. It is set in place again but I think the supports are not in true line with the axis of the chapel. . . . The hanging behind the side altar is up but I think bright (gold or silver) side panels would help."[16] In the original plan all interior walls would have been of sandstone, like the exterior, but Meem decided that the result would be too dark and in the end the side walls were coated with stucco or plaster. There is a stone floor.

Although the mission school has been closed and the hospital has been supplanted by a modern government facility, the church continues to serve a large congregation, almost all members of the Navajo nation. In 2004 the resident chaplain, the Rev. Dr. James Leehan, obtained funding for a major restoration of the church and other buildings at Good Shepherd Mission, and plans were made to celebrate the fiftieth anniversary of Meem's church.

CONCLUSION

JOHN GAW MEEM had a special love of churches and a special talent for designing them. He possessed an exceptional understanding of the relationship between liturgy and space, the intersection between religion, art, and history. His own family background was relevant. Not only was his father an Episcopal missionary; he himself was active for many years at the Church of the Holy Faith in Santa Fe and in the affairs of the Episcopal diocese of New Mexico and the Rio Grande and his wife Faith was also one of the church's leaders.

Throughout his career Meem was by far the most active architect designing Episcopal churches in New Mexico. Even after his retirement he was an advisor to the bishops; as he said, he would not criticize the work of others, but he could comment on the quality and suitability of proposed designs. Roman Catholic archbishops, especially Rudolph Gerken, also sought Meem's advice about new buildings as well as employing him to stabilize St. Francis Cathedral and design Cristo Rey. As we have seen, Meem worked for Presbyterians, Lutherans, and Baptists as well as Episcopalians and Catholics. His plans were often revised over a period of years to accommodate problems of funding. He was always involved in the details of design, construction, and furnishing, and he often became a personal friend of the clergy and lay leaders with whom he worked. He frequently reduced his fees to assist churches in financing fine buildings and sometimes made personal contributions, such as stained-glass windows.

More than his houses or public buildings, Meem's churches fall into a variety of styles. The earliest and largest group may be termed the Spanish Pueblo churches.[1] These were inspired by the great mission church at Acoma, which Meem helped to restore during the 1920s. He assisted with the restoration of a number of other old churches, including those at Laguna and Las Trampas; he gave advice about the churches or chapels at Paraje and Acomita; and he provided designs for similar new churches at McCarty's and Abiquiú. His best-known building in this tradition is, of course, Cristo Rey, the great church in Santa Fe, which is often regarded as the typical expression of his ecclesiastical work. The First Presbyterian Church of Santa Fe also has Pueblo characteristics, although it is less dependent on the Acoma precedent. Several smaller churches, similar to each other, were also designed in this style. These include the Taylor Memorial Chapel in Colorado Springs, the Presbyterian Church in Taos, St. James's Episcopal Church in Clovis, Immanuel Lutheran Church in Santa Fe, and the Alumni Chapel at the University of New Mexico. These buildings were conceived and erected throughout Meem's career, which ranged from 1930 to 1960.

All of these churches appear to be constructed of adobe, although actual building techniques vary. Traditional bricks, made by hand of mud and straw and then sun dried, were used at Cristo Rey and Clovis. The façades generally include a balcony above the principal entrance. Roofs are flat, concealed by a low parapet and not visible from the exterior. There may be a corner bell tower, as at Cristo Rey, or in lesser churches a central turret housing one or more bells. Windows are small simple rectangles holding clear, rather than stained, glass. The altar is brightly lighted by a clerestory window inserted between the lofty sanctuary and the lower nave, not visible to worshipers. Ceilings are made of heavy wooden beams or *vigas*. Elaborately carved corbels support the beams. Carved decoration may be found in other areas as well, sometimes as part of a balcony, as at Cristo Rey and Santa Fe Presbyterian Church. Interiors are simple but may include an important reredos, cross or crucifix, or panel of *retablos*. In addition to the church proper, the buildings may include offices, classrooms, meeting rooms, and a kitchen.

Meem also worked in the Spanish Territorial style. He was requested to do so by the leaders at Immanuel Presbyterian Church in Albuquerque, who were impressed by some of his secular buildings that were based on the Territorial tradition. There was no single inspiration for these churches—nothing comparable to Acoma for the Pueblo-style buildings. In Territorial buildings such as Immanuel, the flat roofs are edged by a red brick coping and supported by steel girders. Commercially fired bricks, rather than handmade sun-dried ones, are used. The exterior is covered with stucco. Wood trim is evident, especially in entrances and window surrounds. The interior walls of the church proper are painted a warm color and have wood paneling. There are elaborately designed tin light fixtures, not concealed lighting as in the Pueblo churches. At Immanuel the entrance leads to a large lobby rather than into the church proper. A square tower crowned by a wooden lookout stage is an important identifying mark that can be seen from some distance. All of these features were part of the original designs for Immanuel, dating from the 1940s, though the building was erected in three stages and not completed until 1956. The Territorial style, verging on the baroque, may also be seen in Meem's expansion of St. Andrew's Episcopal Church in Las Cruces.

Episcopal churches were more likely to be built in the Gothic style, no doubt because of their relationship to medieval churches in England. St. John's Cathedral in Albuquerque is the outstanding example of such work. Here it was originally thought that an earlier building, now too small for the congregation, might be retained and enlarged, but in the end it was decided to demolish most of the old structure and start afresh. The resulting building reminds one of a great thirteenth-century church in the Early English style. The lofty nave is lit by simple pointed windows filled with fine stained glass that casts beautifully colored rays throughout the interior. The building incorporates an existing stone tower but the new work is in brick, chosen because it was less expensive than stone. In the interior the brick is covered with plaster, and one hardly realizes what the structural material is. There is a finely detailed wood ceiling. The long nave is ideally suited to liturgical processions; sight lines and acoustics are excellent. Meem's friendship with the dean of the cathedral, Lloyd Clarke, made the years of designing and building a happy time for both men. The new building was dedicated in 1952.

Meem's own parish church, Holy Faith in Santa Fe, faced a similar problem. Here again the original church, built in 1882, was no longer adequate. In Santa Fe, however, it was decided to retain the historic structure as the nave and add a new sanctuary. This was completed in 1954. As in Albuquerque, it is lit by three lancet windows above the altar and several more on the side, again filled with stained glass commissioned by Meem and (as at the cathedral) partly paid for by him as a memorial to his father. The wood ceiling is more elaborately detailed than that in the nave, but the two styles are harmonious and the building possesses a greater unity than might be expected, considering the decades that separate the two parts of the church.

A few years earlier Meem had added a new chancel to St. Paul's Episcopal Church in Las Vegas. The original stone structure here had been built in 1886, at a time when Las Vegas was flourishing because of the advent of the Santa Fe railroad, which ironically bypassed Santa Fe itself. Meem's new altar is once again surmounted by three lancet windows filled with stained glass, this time made in Philadelphia by a firm that had worked at the National Cathedral. The Gothic style can also be seen in the Episcopal churches at Roswell and Carlsbad. In both cases Meem made additions to earlier buildings. St. Andrew's Church in Roswell was rebuilt and expanded in 1950. The exterior is a combination of stone courses near the ground and less expensive stucco above, with a half-timbered entrance porch that is another reminder of English influence. In Carlsbad a historic building dating from 1890 was retained as the nave; in 1952 Meem added a choir, sanctuary, sacristy, and priest's study. Here too there is some half-timbering as well as stone on the exterior.

Finally there are two unique churches, each in a style of its own. As we have seen, Meem originally thought that the Spanish Pueblo vernacular might be appropriate for the Catholic cathedral in Gallup, as it had been at Cristo Rey, but the building that he eventually erected was an essay in the Romanesque, as inspired by early medieval churches in France or Spain. It may be that this style was dictated by a bishop and other church leaders who had European backgrounds. In any case, Meem made the style his own and added his own touches, including the use of brick rather than stone (once again, because of financial considerations) and the attachment of a regional style porch or portal.

It is the last of his great churches that is the most personal. The Good Shepherd Mission at Fort Defiance is unlike any other church designed by Meem or any other architect. It is not based on any existing tradition but rather possesses a style all its own. It relates in a special way to the countryside where it was built and to the fact that it was to be used by members of the Navajo nation, not by descendants of European immigrants. It uses native stone and other materials. Even more exceptional is the use of aluminum ornamentation, a tribute to the financial sponsorship of Arthur Vining Davis. Its tower, window grills, and crucifix are unlike those anywhere else. It is as if John Gaw Meem, having worked with exceptional skill in a number of styles borrowed from others, had made a final personal statement that was wholly his own.

John Gaw Meem died in 1983 at age eighty-eight.

NOTES

ONE: EARLY WORK, 1926–1939

1. For earlier accounts of Meem's life see Bainbridge Bunting, *John Gaw Meem: Southwestern Architect* (Albuquerque: University of New Mexico Press, 1983), 3–14; Beatrice Chauvenet, *John Gaw Meem, Pioneer in Historic Preservation* (Santa Fe: Museum of New Mexico Press, 1985), 3–24; and Chris Wilson, *Facing Southwest: The Life and Houses of John Gaw Meem* (New York: Norton, 2001), 5–15.
2. Cf. Carl D. Sheppard, *Creator of the Santa Fe Style: Isaac Hamilton Rapp* (Albuquerque: University of New Mexico Press, 1988).
3. See Stanford Lehmberg, *Holy Faith of Santa Fe, 1863–2000* (Albuquerque: LPD Press, 2004), 60–1. Materials relating to the construction of Palen Hall are in the Meem Job Files, Southwest Research Center, Zimmerman Library, University of New Mexico, boxes 12 and 12B.
4. Meem Job Files, box 4, folder 20.
5. Shonnard died in her nineties in 1978.
6. On the history of Acoma see Ward Alan Minge, *Acoma: Pueblo in the Sky* (Albuquerque: University of New Mexico Press, 1976); L. Bradford Prince, *Spanish Mission Churches of New Mexico* (reprint, Glorieta, NM: Rio Grande Press, 1977), 214–25; George Kubler, *The Religious Architecture of New Mexico* (Albuquerque: University of New Mexico Press, 1940), passim; John L. Kessell, *The Missions of New Mexico since 1776* (Albuquerque: University of New Mexico Press, 1980), passim.
7. Chauvenet, 30–1. The *canales* were openings or spouts that drained water from the roof.
8. Quoted in Chauvenet, 35.

9. Chauvenet, 41. The church at Acoma has been restored several more times since Meem's work. The most recent project, underway in 2003, is partly sponsored by Cornerstones, a Santa Fe organization founded by Nancy Meem Worth.

10. Correspondence in Meem Job Files, box 10, folder 200.

11. Ibid.

12. The specifications, dated March 1, 1935, are in the Meem Job Files, box 17, folder 33. For the history of the area and its church, see Leslie Poling-Kempes, *Valley of Shining Stone: The Story of Abiquiú* (Tucson: University of Arizona Press, 1997), esp. 149–52.

13. See Chauvenet, 61–9; the photograph is reproduced on the dust jacket of Chauvenet's book.

14. Chauvenet, 43–59.

15. Meem Job Files, box 17, folder 248.

16. Meem Job Files, box 10, folder 29.

17. It is interesting that the committee had said that the appearance of the building was to be "in no way ecclesiastical." See Bunting, 78–86.

18. Meem Job Files, box 18, folders 251 (correspondence and bills) and 251A (photographs of the deteriorated footings and arcades). See also Bruce Ellis, *Bishop Lamy's Santa Fe Cathedral* (Albuquerque: University of New Mexico Press, 1985), 147.

19. Francisco Atanasio Domínguez, *The Missions of New Mexico*, 1776, eds. Eleanor B. Adams and Fray Angelico Chavez (Albuquerque: University of New Mexico Press, 1956), 34–5, quoted in Chauvenet, 76. See also A. Von Wuthenau, "The Spanish Military Chapels in Santa Fe and the Reredos of Our Lady of Light," *New Mexico Historical Review* X (July 1935): 175–94.

20. Rev. Daniel W. Krahe, *Cristo Rey: A Symphony in Mud* (Albuquerque: Lourdes School Press, 1940), 27.

21. Meem Job Files, box 17, folder 248.

22. Interview with Alfonso Trujillo, August 2004.

23. Krahe, 48–51.

24. Meem Job Files, box 2:25, folder 315. It might be noted that the reredos now rests on a polychrome rock foundation that was not designed or approved by Meem. See Bunting, 127–8.

25. Ibid.

26. Meem Job Files, box 2:25, folder 315.

27. Chauvenet, 87.

28. Paul A. F. Walter, quoted in Chauvenet, 87.

29. There is a history of the church—T. D. Allen, *Not Ordered by Men* (Santa Fe: Rydal Press, 1967)—but it does not discuss Meem's work.

30. This and the following quotations are taken from a speech given at the church by Meem on April 29, 1973; copy in the Meem Job Files, box 23, folder 297.

TWO: THE MIDDLE YEARS, 1940–1951

1. This historical information is drawn from an essay by Dr. Myra Ellen Jenkins in a pamphlet, "A Century of Living Faith," published by the Cathedral Church of St. John in 1982. There is a copy in the Meem Job Files, box 4, folder 32.

2. Meem Job Files, box 4, folder 33.

3. Materials related to St. John's are in the Meem Job Files, box 25, folder 318-B.

4. Bainbridge Bunting, *John Gaw Meem, Southwestern Architect* (Albuquerque: University of New Mexico Press, 1983), 117.

5. Meem Job Files, box 25, folder 318B.

6. Meem Job Files, box 25, folder 318A.

7. Meem Papers, box 3, folder 14. This file also includes an amusing letter from Dean Haverland thanking Meem for the $5,000 check that completed the pledge he and Faith had made to the cathedral building fund, but noting that Meem had forgotten to sign it.

8. On Meem's work at Holy Faith see Stanford Lehmberg, *Holy Faith of Santa Fe, 1863–2000* (Albuquerque: LPD Press, 2004), 79–88.

9. A friend of Meem, Baumann had joined with Will Shuster in fabricating the first Zozobra for the Santa Fe fiesta in 1926. An illustrated pamphlet was issued at the time of the dedication of the reredos; there are copies in the parish office.

10. Meem Papers, box 3, folders 25 and 27.

11. I am grateful to Cameron Mactavish for this anecdote and other information and to Dorothy Brandenburg and her daughter, Barbara Brenner, for their memories of the project. When interviewed in January 2004 at the age of 101, Mrs. Brandenburg still had distinct recollections of Meem and was appreciative of his willingness to forgo the usual architect's fees. Her father was the painter Oscar E. Berninghaus, one of the founders of the Taos Society of Artists. See Dean A. Porter, Theresa Hayes Ebie, and Susan Campbell, *Taos Artists and Their Patrons, 1898–1950* (Notre Dame: Snite Museum of Art, 1949), passim.

12. Meem Job Files, box 27, folders 371 and 371A; Bunting, 120–5.

13. It is not clear to which of Meem's buildings the members referred. He had indeed employed the Territorial Revival style in several governmental buildings in Santa Fe, including the Federal Emergency Recovery Building (or FERA, 1934, now called the Villagra Building) and the Santa Fe Municipal Building (1936), but not in earlier churches. See Chris Wilson, *The Myth of Santa Fe* (Albuquerque: University of New Mexico Press, 1997), 281–2.

14. I am greatly indebted to Eleanor Mitchell for information about the building history at Immanuel Presbyterian Church. A principal source at the church is Gertrude Hogg and others, "35 Forward in Faith—History of Immanuel Presbyterian Church," unpublished manuscript, 1983. Meem's materials are in Meem Job Files, box 56, folders 557 and 557I. These include drawings and correspondence with the M. P. Möller organ company.

15. Meem Job Files, box 27, folder 358. There is a short parish history: Alice Young, "Flower of the High Plains: Church of St. James the Apostle, 1909–1999."

16. A freestanding altar was installed in 1993; it was made by 85-year-old James Ridgeley Whiteman, the craftsman who had made the pulpit and lectern for Meem. The cross that Meem placed over the altar has now been moved to a side wall, and an Italian figure of the Risen Christ, purchased in 1997, hangs in its place.

17. Meem Job Files, box 53, folder 490.

18. Meem Job Files, box 53, folder 513. I am grateful to the church for sending me copies of rel-

evant entries from its archives; these entries suggest that it was Hugo Zehner of Meem's office who worked directly with the church.

19. Meem Job Files, box 23, folder 292. In 1991, following national agreements between the Episcopal and Lutheran churches, St. Paul's joined with the Peace Lutheran Church to form the present St. Paul's Peace Church.
20. Meem Job Files, box 56, folder 556.
21. Details of the work in Roswell may be found in "A History of St. Andrew's Church" by Edith Wolf Standhardt, compiled in 1966, copies of which are in the church office. See also Meem Job Files, box 55, folder 548. Meem did not supervise the construction himself—that was done by a local architect, E. C. French—and he was not responsible for the later additions to the building. A fine organ made by the Gene R. Bedint company was installed at St. Andrew's in 1978.

THREE: THE LAST DECADE, 1952–1960

1. Meem Job Files, box 39, folder 397.
2. The final plans and drawings, dated 1954, are in the Job Files, folders 397A–R. Amazingly detailed, they include specifications of paint colors, plumbing, heating, woodwork, electrical fixtures, mosaic floors, roofing, fire extinguishers, insurance, and a sound system. Kinney common brick was used. The contractor was Dan Brunetta.
3. There is a separate file on the chapel (not part of the Meem papers) in the Southwest Research Center at the university.
4. Meem Job Files, box 61, folder 603. The files include correspondence with the Wicks Organ Company.
5. Information from an interview with the Rev. Al Tarbell, October 2003. Job Files, box 63, folder 640 includes correspondence from 1957 and 1961. The last stages of this project, following Meem's retirement from active practice, were handled by Edward Holien.
6. Job Files, box 61, folder 613, and historical materials provided by the parish. See also James M. Stoney, *Lighting the Candle* (Santa Fe: Rydal Press, 1961), for information about Bishop Kendrick and "Preacher" Hunter Lewis, who also worked at Mesilla and Las Cruces. Because still more space was needed to serve the growing congregation, an addition of nearly 7,000 square feet was added to the north and east sides of the church about 2000. It was designed by the architect Robert D. Habiger and received an award for its success in adhering to regional architecture.
7. Information from the program for the eighty-fifth anniversary worship service on August 25, 2002, kindly provided by Pastor Ted With.
8. See Willow Roberts Powers, *Navajo Trading: The End of an Era* (Albuquerque: University of New Mexico Press, 2001), 26–8 and passim.
9. Kinsolving's letter, along with a great deal of additional correspondence and plans, is in the Meem Job Files, box 59, folder 584. The files, folders 584A–R, continue in box 60. There are also a large number of drawings and blueprints showing details of the window grills, tower, pulpit, and lectern as well as plumbing, electrical work, and a boiler house.

10. The Arthur Vining Davis Foundation later made a grant of $100,000 to the Navajo Community College (subsequently known as Dineh College) to initiate a study of the Navajo philosophy of learning.

11. There is a special Meem connection here, for the Meems' daughter Nancy married John Wirth, whose father had been a master at the Ranch School. A distinguished Latin American historian who taught at Stanford, Wirth collaborated on a history of the school shortly before his death: John D. Wirth and Linda Harvey Aldrich, *Los Alamos: The Ranch School Years, 1917–1943* (Albuquerque: University of New Mexico Press, 2003).

12. Davis Given to Stanford Lehmberg, 2003. One of those who worked with Fr. Given in the 1950s was the New Mexico historian Marc Simmons, who, like Given, had been attracted to the reservation by his interest in the Navajo and the scenery. During the summer of 1954 Simmons served as an acolyte at the mission, and ten years later, while working as a horse wrangler at the Los Piños Ranch on the Upper Pecos River, he met Given again and took him for "a strenuous all-day horseback ride to Truchas Lake, deep in the Wilderness." Simmons very kindly shared his reminiscences and some photographs with me in December 2003.

13. Given to Lehmberg, 2003. I am very grateful to Fr. Given for sending me information and comments about Fort Defiance and for several valuable telephone conversations. In these he stressed his personal friendship with John and Faith Meem; on several occasions when he felt he needed some time away from the Navajo reservation he and his wife spent a few days in Santa Fe as guests in the Meems' home. After leaving Good Shepherd (he would have been happy to spend his entire life there, he said) he returned to New York, where he served as a hospital chaplain and a member of the clerical staff at Trinity Church, Wall Street (a position about as different from that at the mission as one could imagine).

14. It is interesting to note that Meem had used aluminum during the 1930s in the Colorado Springs Fine Arts Center. In addition to aluminum light fixtures, it has cast aluminum window and ventilator grills incorporating stylized Native American patterns. He also designed aluminum grills for the First National Bank in Santa Fe.

15. Job Files, box 59, folder 584A–R.

16. Job Files, box 59, folder 584.

CONCLUSION

1. The descriptor was used by Meem and by Bainbridge Bunting, *John Gaw Meem, Southwestern Architect* (Albuquerque: University of New Mexico Press, 1983), 117.

CREDITS

Except as noted below, all color photographs were taken by Derek Lehmberg in 2003 and 2004. Black-and-white photographs not otherwise identified are by Tyler Dingee and date from 1945 to 1961. These are part of the John Gaw Meem Archives in the Center for Southwest Research, Zimmerman Library, University of New Mexico, and are reproduced by kind permission of the center and the copyright holder, Nancy Meem Wirth.

Other illustrations:

Nos. 15–17, 27, 28, 31, 34, 35, 43, 45, 49–52, 61, 70, 77, 81, 83, 88, 90, 94, drawings and studies from the Meem Archives, Center for Southwest Research, reproduced by permission.

No. 3, photograph by Tyler Dingee, Museum of New Mexico photo archives, neg. no. 0719, reprinted by permission.

Nos. 99, 100, photographs by Marc Simmons, courtesy Marc Simmons.

Photographs of the interior of Cristo Rey Church are reproduced by permission of the archivist of the Archdiocese of Santa Fe.

INDEX